MIGHTY ROAR

The Story of the 2019 Memphis Tigers Football Team

commercial appeal

PART OF THE USA TODAY NETWORK

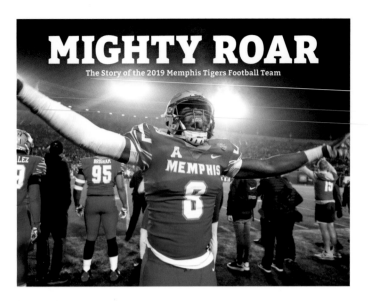

MIGHTY ROAR

The Story of the 2019 Memphis Tigers Football Team

On the cover

FRONT COVER: Memphis Tigers linebacker Xavier Cullens celebrates their 29-24 AAC Championship win over Cincinnati at the Liberty Bowl Memorial Stadium.

JOE RONDONE / THE COMMERCIAL APPEAL

Copyright © 2020 by The Commercial Appeal
All Rights Reserved • ISBN: 978-1-59725-905-7

No part of this book may be reproduced, stored in a retrieval system or transmitted in any form or by any means, electronic, mechanical, photocopying, recording or otherwise, without prior written permission of the copyright owner or the publisher.

Published by Pediment Publishing, a division of The Pediment Group, Inc. • www.pediment.com
Printed in Canada.

Credits

A product of The Commercial Appeal

Mark Russell   EXECUTIVE EDITOR

Dann Miller   SENIOR CONSUMER EXPERIENCE DIRECTOR

Tommy Deas   SPORTS DIRECTOR TENNESSEE-FLORIDA REGION, USA TODAY NETWORK

Stories

Evan Barnes   TIGERS FOOTBALL BEAT WRITER

Mark Giannotto   SPORTS COLUMNIST

Jason Munz   SPORTS WRITER

Photography

Joe Rondone

Max Gersh

Ariel Cobbert

Henry Taylor

USA TODAY Sports Images

The Associated Press

Table of Contents

4   The Rise of a Program

6   Honors and Awards

9   Preseason

13   Ole Miss

25   Southern

31   South Alabama

37   Navy

45   Louisiana-Monroe

51   Temple

59   Tulane

65   Tulsa

75   ESPN College GameDay

85   SMU

99   Houston

105 South Florida

111 Cincinnati

125 American Athletic Conference (AAC) Championship Game

143 Mike Norvell's Legacy

147 Cotton Bowl

160 Afterword

The rise of a program and an end to suffering

BY MARK GIANNOTTO • THE COMMERCIAL APPEAL

> ## "One day we're going to have a good team and we're going to forget about this day."
>
> JASON RHEA

When Jason Rhea tailgated before one of the great moments in Memphis football history, and even when he sat in Liberty Bowl Memorial Stadium during one of the great moments in Memphis football history, he kept coming back to the moment he promised himself he'd forget.

What year it happened and who it happened against — he thinks it was ECU — have faded with time. But Rhea, 42, remembers it was raining out, there were less than 1,000 fans in the stands at kickoff, and he and some friends sat through another loss thinking, "I never thought it would get this bad."

"One day we're going to have a good team and we're going to forget about this day," he told himself then.

So this year, when Memphis had a great team, a team on the verge of history, Rhea and those same friends were tailgating outside the Liberty Bowl ahead of the American Athletic Conference (AAC) Championship Game. And they talked about when it hurt to be a Memphis football fan, when it seemed like a season like this one seemed so far fetched, and what it would feel like to win a title.

"Actually, it makes it way better," Rhea said.

It's what happened before this historic Memphis football season, and what it took for this program to reach this point, that made everything that happened in the fall of 2019 so memorable. This wasn't just the first outright conference championship in 50 years for Memphis. This was the climax of a program resurrection that began at the beginning of this decade.

Because before Memphis set a new program record for wins, before it set a new record for consecutive weeks ranked in the national polls, before it could earn a spot in the most prestigious bowl game in program history, it had to occupy the literal bottom of Division-I football. It had to rise up under Justin Fuente and fall short in AAC championship games under Mike Norvell.

The Tigers' long-suffering fans had to suffer, and it's why this season featured so much joy. Just think about the memories created, memories that will live on forever because of what was accomplished in the end.

There was the dramatic safety by defensive lineman Bryce Huff that sealed the season-opening win against Ole Miss, the first sign that this Tigers' defense would be different.

Then came the 73-yard touchdown pass on third-and-13 from quarterback Brady White to wide receiver Antonio Gibson, not long after White had been booed by some of the home crowd. This spurred White and Gibson the rest of the season. Norvell, meanwhile, called this his favorite moment ahead of the Tigers' AAC championship game win over Cincinnati.

The only loss, at Temple, featured a questionable replay reversal that Memphis fans will talk about for years to come — "Joey caught the ball!" — because it prevented an undefeated season. But Tulsa's missed kick the following week saved the season and brought ESPN's "College GameDay" to Memphis the next week.

That day, when fans filled Beale Street in the morning and filled the Liberty Bowl at night, became an unforgettable symbol of the heights this program was approaching.

And they were reached with back-to-back wins over Cincinnati, and the latter one featured a confetti-filled scene on the field that made Norvell's impending departure to Florida State an afterthought. Fans of every generation were out there celebrating, not just the championship but what had happened to get it.

Rhea, for instance, sat in those same seats with his wife, watching his children revel and trying to savor what he'd been through to get here.

He started a Facebook group right after Justine Fuente got hired, right

after what he called "the literal bottom," when Memphis football fans were slow to embrace their new football coach. Once Fuente left, Rhea turned it into a group simply dedicated to Memphis Tiger football, regardless of the coach. As the wins piled up, "it just took on a life of its own," he said.

This season, it grew to more than 16,300 members.

Because this season is a lot different than the moment he assumed he'd forget. This season is a moment we'll never forget.

To the victors go the spoils

Memphis reaped the rewards of a historic 2019 season.
Here's a list of all the awards won by the Tigers:

ANTONIO GIBSON

» AAC co-Special Teams Player of the Year
» First-team All-AAC kick returner
» Second-team All-AAC wide receiver
» Joe Allison co-Special Teams Players of the Year
» Memphis Most Improved Player of the Year (offense)

KENNETH GAINWELL

» AAC Rookie of the Year
» First-team Freshman All-American (The Athletic)
» First-team All-AAC running back (unanimous selection)
» First-team Midseason All-American (Sporting News)
» Second-team Midseason All-American (Associated Press, The Athletic)

» Second-team All-American (Sporting News, AFCA)
» Isaac Bruce co-Offensive Player of the Year

RILEY PATTERSON

» First-team All-AAC kicker
» Joe Allison co-Special Teams Players of the Year

DAMONTE COXIE

» Second-team All-AAC wide receiver
» Isaac Bruce Co-Offensive Player of the Year

BRYCE HUFF

» Second-team All-AAC defensive line

JOEY MAGNIFICO

» Second-team All-AAC tight end

BRADY WHITE

» Second-team All-AAC quarterback
» DeAngelo Williams Most Valuable Player

DUSTIN WOODARD

» Second-team All-AAC offensive line
» True Tiger Award

T.J. CARTER

» Honorable mention All-AAC defensive back

JOSEPH DORCEUS

» Honorable mention All-AAC defensive line

O'BRYAN GOODSON

» Honorable mention All-AAC defensive line

AUSTIN HALL

» Honorable mention All-AAC linebacker

» John Bramlett Defensive Player of the Year

DYLAN PARHAM

» Honorable mention All-AAC offensive line

SANCHEZ BLAKE

» Memphis Most Improved Player of the Year (defense)

PATRICK TAYLOR

» True Tiger Award

ASA MARTIN

» Scout Team Offensive Player of the Year

KENDALL JOHNSON

» Scout Team co-Defensive Player of the Year

CADE MASHBURN

» Scout Team co-Defensive Player of the Year

JA'LEN SIMS

» Scout Team Special Teams Player of the Year

Goal for season?
Get 1 percent better

BY EVAN BARNES • THE COMMERCIAL APPEAL

MEMPHIS - Before the 2019 season, Mike Norvell didn't publicly state any goals for his Memphis team. He had no talk of an AAC championship or a New Year's Six bowl game.

The only change was the slogan of being 1% better: Continue to improve each practice and build on what Memphis had already accomplished in his first three seasons.

He talked of the Tigers being a coach-inspired, player-led group. It was a reminder of how in 2018 the Tigers finished 8-6, but after eight games Norvell was still looking for leaders to emerge.

With a veteran group in 2019, he knew players would hold each other more accountable. But how would that translate on the field? While the Tigers were picked by the media to win the AAC West and one offshore betting site had projected them to be favored in every game, there were real questions entering the season?

How would Memphis replace two running backs in Darrell Henderson and Tony Pollard, who were both drafted in April? How would a Memphis offensive line — the only Group of Five finalist for the 2018 Joe Moore Award handed to the nation's best line — replace three starters while moving all-conference guard Dustin Woodard to center?

Would Brady White improve after an inconsistent first year at quarterback? Could the Tigers' defense — one of the nation's best at creating takeaways from 2016–18 — improve from being a liability to an asset?

How would the Memphis staff gel together with seven new assistants, including three new coordinators?

Even if the Tigers won the West for a third straight season, could they finally win that AAC championship that eluded them in 2017 and 2018? Twice, UCF had ended their dreams in heartbreaking fashion, including overcoming a 17-point halftime deficit the season before.

Those were the mysteries surrounding Memphis at the start of Norvell's fourth season. Few knew what to expect, but with a season opener against Ole Miss, the Tigers and their fans would find out soon if 2019 would be a different type of year.

OPPOSITE: Brady White throws the ball during a drill as the Memphis Tigers Football team holds its first fall practice at the Billy J. Murphy Athletic Complex on Aug 2, 2019. JOE RONDONE / THE COMMERCIAL APPEAL

RIGHT: Kedarian Jones signals out to his teammates during a drill.
JOE RONDONE / THE COMMERCIAL APPEAL

ABOVE FAR RIGHT: Linebackers coach Kevin Clune. JOE RONDONE / THE COMMERCIAL APPEAL

ABOVE RIGHT: Kylan Watkins.
JOE RONDONE / THE COMMERCIAL APPEAL

LEFT: Pop Williams.
JOE RONDONE / THE COMMERCIAL APPEAL

BELOW LEFT: Patrick Taylor Jr.
JOE RONDONE / THE COMMERCIAL APPEAL

BELOW: Antonio Gibson.
JOE RONDONE / THE COMMERCIAL APPEAL

Memphis defense changes narrative in opener

BY EVAN BARNES • THE COMMERCIAL APPEAL

It was gut-check time for the Memphis defense, a unit that's been criticized for two seasons for not getting timely stops.

Adam Williams punted the ball to the Ole Miss 2. It was an opportunity to change the narrative, and Bryce Huff did that by racing untouched to sack Matt Corral for a safety.

It helped Memphis survive for a 15-10 win over Ole Miss and spark a wild celebration at the Liberty Bowl. It wasn't the monumental upset the Tigers had over Ole Miss in 2015, but it was still a satisfying, big win over an SEC opponent

Here's what we learned from Memphis' fourth consecutive season-opening win under coach Mike Norvell.

Memphis' defense is improved

New coordinator Adam Fuller promised a swarming unit that creates pressure. It showed by the Tigers holding Ole Miss to 173 total yards.

Ole Miss finished 1-for-10 on third down, and no defensive play was bigger than Huff's safety with 6:27 remaining. Memphis finished with 10 tackles for loss, including sacks by La'Andre Thomas and Joseph Dorceus.

Patrick Taylor, who moved into third place on Memphis' all-time rushing list, had 128 rushing yards before limping off during the game's final drive. Kenneth Gainwell dazzled in his first start with 118 all-purpose yards.

The Tigers' passing game? Not so explosive. Brady White was 23 of 31 for 172 yards as he and the offensive line struggled most of the game.

Quindell Johnson makes big first impression

The redshirt freshman made his debut at safety after La'Andre Thomas was ejected for targeting just before the end of the first quarter. It didn't take long for him to look comfortable.

Johnson got his first interception by reading a pass perfectly and caught it before he fell out of bounds. The Tigers may have retired the takeaway robe and belt, but Johnson being mobbed by his teammates felt just as good.

Penalties rear their ugly head again

Memphis had 10 penalties and at least three of them stalled drives in Ole Miss territory. Right guard Manuel Orona-Lopez, in his first start, drew four false-start flags.

It was another reminder the Tigers have been a heavily penalized team in the Norvell era.

OPPOSITE: Memphis Tigers defensive end Bryce Huff (55) celebrates after sacking Ole Miss quarterback Matt Corral for a safety at Liberty Bowl Memorial Stadium on Aug. 31, 2019. JUSTIN FORD / USA TODAY SPORTS

ABOVE: Memphis Tigers running back Traveon Samuel charges out on the field with his teammates before their game against Ole Miss. JOE RONDONE / THE COMMERCIAL APPEAL

RIGHT: Memphis Tigers players run out on the field before their game against Ole Miss. JOE RONDONE / THE COMMERCIAL APPEAL

RIGHT: Memphis Tigers defender JJ Russell tackles Ole Miss running back Scottie Phillips. JOE RONDONE / THE COMMERCIAL APPEAL

OPPOSITE: Memphis Tigers tight end Joey Magnifico celebrates a touchdown by teammate Brady White against Ole Miss. JOE RONDONE / THE COMMERCIAL APPEAL

BELOW RIGHT: Memphis Tigers running back Kenneth Gainwell celebrates following a play against Ole Miss. JOE RONDONE / THE COMMERCIAL APPEAL

BELOW: Memphis Tigers running back Kenneth Gainwell dives just short of the end zone. JOE RONDONE / THE COMMERCIAL APPEAL

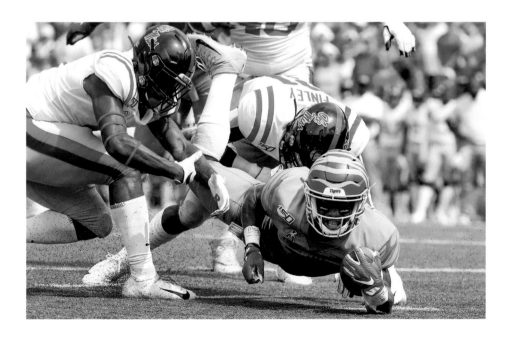

Tigers build brand with win over Ole Miss

BY MARK GIANNOTTO • THE COMMERCIAL APPEAL

> **"The mission was to grow it to be like this. You're here to see it in fruition. This is special."**
>
> ISAAC BRUCE

Isaac Bruce stopped posing for pictures with his old Memphis State teammates, raised his arm in the air and took in the roar of the student section. It was about 30 minutes before kickoff and the 2019 Memphis football team came running toward the corner of Liberty Bowl Memorial Stadium to rile up the crowd.

This moment, hours before the defining image of Tiger defensive end Bryce Huff flying into the backfield for the game-changing safety, was not lost on one of the program's all-time greats.

"The mission was to grow it to be like this," said Bruce. "You're here to see it in fruition. This is special. The brand is definitely growing."

The brand is to the point that Memphis' 15-10 win over Ole Miss while worth celebrating, didn't feel like an upset (and it wasn't according to the oddsmakers).

It's to the point that the self-proclaimed Big Brother (Ole Miss) in this series won't play Little Brother for the foreseeable future because Little Brother keeps putting a damper on Big Brother's season.

It's to the point that Memphis overpowered an SEC team using an entirely different formula than we've all grown accustomed to, and some Tiger fans left grousing about all the things that didn't go right for the home team.

That's what we call first-world problems. At least for Week 1.

"We're their little brothers, but … as people get older, the little brother starts to get the better of the big brother," Huff said.

Here's what else became obvious once Saturday concluded:

The Memphis defense looked much better under new coordinator Adam Fuller and saved the Tigers from another second-half collapse.

The Memphis offense looked much worse without Darrell Henderson and Tony Pollard, running behind a new offensive line.

The quarterback — Brady White — looked just as shaky as he did at the end of last season.

And, in case you've forgotten already, the Tigers still beat Ole Miss.

Even after a wave of starters went down to injury.

Even after they nearly blew a 13-0 halftime lead.

Were there concerns? Of course.

Ole Miss might be the worst team in the SEC this year. And Memphis couldn't put the Rebels away, despite controlling long portions of the game.

Despite Norvell's preseason rhetoric, White's sporadic play remains an issue — particularly now that he's playing behind an offensive line that committed a bevy of pre-snap penalties and struggled to contain the Ole Miss pass rush.

But when it mattered most, when the game seemed to be slipping from the Tigers' grip, this revamped defense didn't wither like so many of Memphis' recent defenses have.

They held Ole Miss to minus-1 rushing yard in the first half. They allowed just 173 yards for the entire game. Ole Miss went 1-of-10 on third down. And then, with the Tigers nursing a 13-10 lead in the fourth quarter, Huff burst through the line untouched and slammed quarterback Matt Corral to the end zone turf.

It was the first safety by a Memphis defense since the 2015 season, and it feels much longer than that since the Tigers have been propelled to a win without their prolific offense leading the way.

Even better: Memphis finished off this victory with a 14-play drive that spanned the final 6:21 of the fourth quarter and included a fourth-and-2 conversion from the Ole Miss 47 via a shovel pass to freshman Kenneth Gainwell.

Before the play, Norvell said he spoke to Fuller on his headset and asked what he should do.

"Go win it," Fuller said back, and so that's what the Tigers did.

"You're going to see pictures on the wall of this game," at the team's facility,

Norvell declared during his postgame news conference. "They can come back to Memphis any time they want."

Does it mean Memphis can finally win an AAC title this year? Saturday should probably tamp down any preseason presumptions. But I'll bet on Norvell sorting out the offense over the next few weeks given his track record.

It's the pregame scene, though, that resonated most of all.

Norvell said he got goosebumps on the Tiger walk into the Liberty Bowl. It was incredible on the field, too, filled with happiness and optimism, about this season and about the place Memphis football has elevated itself at the moment.

Bruce came up from his home in South Florida and Pollard was also here. So was American Athletic Conference commissioner Mike Aresco, new athletic director Laird Veatch and FedEx CEO Fred Smith.

They were here to watch a season opener between two rivals — and yes, it's a rivalry if only because Ole Miss fans so often feel compelled to tell us it's not a rivalry.

But they were also here to admire what this program is now.

"This is not your grandfather's Memphis," Aresco said.

Memphis Tigers quarterback Brady White looks to throw against Ole Miss.

JOE RONDONE / THE COMMERCIAL APPEAL

ABOVE: Memphis wide receiver Kedarian Jones celebrates after the Tigers defeat Ole Miss.
ARIEL COBBERT / THE COMMERCIAL APPEAL

ABOVE LEFT: Memphis Tigers running back Kenneth Gainwell carries the ball. JOE RONDONE / THE COMMERCIAL APPEAL

LEFT: Memphis Tigers running back Patrick Taylor Jr. carries the ball. JOE RONDONE / THE COMMERCIAL APPEAL

Sports

MEMPHIS 15, OLE MISS 10

Satisfying start

Memphis wide receiver Kedarian Jones (13) celebrates after the Tigers defeated Ole Miss 15-10 on Saturday.
ARIEL COBBERT/THE COMMERCIAL APPEAL

5 things learned from Tigers' win over Ole Miss

Evan Barnes Memphis Commercial Appeal
USA TODAY NETWORK – TENNESSEE

It was gut check time for the Memphis defense.

A unit that's been criticized for two seasons for not getting timely stops, Adam Williams punted the ball to the Ole Miss 2.

It was an opportunity to change the narrative, and Bryce Huff did that by racing untouched to sack Matt Corral for a safety.

It helped Memphis survive for 15-10 win over Ole Miss and spark a wild celebration at the Liberty Bowl on Saturday. It wasn't the monumental upset they had over Ole Miss in 2015, but it was still a satisfying, big win over an

SEC opponent.

Here's what we learned from Memphis' fourth consecutive season-opening win under coach Mike Norvell.

Memphis' defense is improved

New defensive coordinator Adam Fuller promised a swarming unit that creates pressure and it showed by the Tigers holding Ole Miss to 173 total yards.

Ole Miss finished 1-for-10 on third down, and no defensive play was bigger than Huff's safety with 6:27 remaining.

Memphis finished with 10 tackles for loss, including sacks by La'Andre Thomas and Joseph Dorceus.

Offense good, not great

Patrick Taylor, who moved into third place on Memphis' all-time rushing list, had 128 rushing yards before limping off the field during the final drive. Kenneth Gainwell dazzled in his first start with 118 all-purpose yards.

The Tigers' passing game? Not so explosive. Brady White was 23-if-31 for just 172 yards as he and the offensive line struggled most of the game.

In the fourth quarter, White managed the game well as he led the Tigers on a six-minute drive to end the game, including a fourth-and-2 shovel pass to Gainwell to keep it alive.

See TIGERS, Page 4B

Father-son duo helps Cordova end Germantown win streak

Khari Thompson Memphis Commercial Appeal
USA TODAY NETWORK – TENNESSEE

During spring practice, Cordova coach Marcus Wimberly was looking for a quarterback. Then he found a familiar face among his linebackers. His son, Cameron Wimberly, volunteered to give it a shot.

"He just said, 'I'll try it dad,' and he's done a tremendous job. He's been making plays. Of course he's going to make some mistakes because he's a rookie at it but it's been satisfying," Marcus Wimberly said.

So far, the father-son duo has proven to be effective as Cordova (2-0, 1-0 8-1A) snapped Germantown's 22 regular-season win streak with a 21-20 road win on Friday. Before Friday, the Red Devils' last regular-season loss was against Cordova in 2016.

Cameron Wimberly, a junior, threw a touchdown pass from 26 yards out to Falandis Norry Jr. in the first quarter. He also scored two touchdowns on the ground.

"Nobody thought we were going to do it. Everybody thought we were going to lose," Cameron Wimberly said. "Everybody thought I wasn't capable. I thank God we were able to prove everybody wrong."

It was also the second close victory in a row for the Wolves, who beat Central 13-12 last week. He rushed for a touchdown in that game and helped lead the Wolves to victory after being shut out in the first half.

"Man he makes plays. Taking off with the ball, doing little cutbacks, throwing

See DUO, Page 5B

Cordova's Cameron Wimberly (3) rolls into the end zone for his second touchdown on Friday.
ARIEL COBBERT/THE COMMERCIAL APPEAL

AAC commish calls for automatic New Year's Six bid

Brady White lights up Southern

BY JASON MUNZ • THE COMMERCIAL APPEAL

Brady White, making his 15th start in a Memphis football uniform, had one of his best games as a Tiger in their second game of the 2019 season.

In a 55-24 victory over Southern, he was 17-of-21 for 337 yards with two touchdown passes. White's 81-percent completion percentage was the second-best single-game mark of his year-plus Memphis career. Those 337 yards through the air (in just three quarters, mind you — he was lifted for backup Connor Adair in the fourth) are the third-most he's had in a game under Mike Norvell.

White's biggest takeaway, however — aside from the win — was more about the yards he didn't rack up. More about the touchdown throws that weren't made. More about the plays, even good ones, that could've been better.

"I think we left a lot on the field," White said. "We're happy we won, but at the same time, I know we can perform at a lot higher level. I'm going to make sure of that this upcoming week. That's a point of emphasis. I'm making sure we're pushing our guys and I'm being a leader in that aspect so that we maximize every opportunity on Saturdays or whenever we're playing."

It's evident White — like every player — still has room to grow and learn. Norvell admitted as much. For as many good things his junior quarterback did, Norvell agreed it could've been better.

"He was very efficient," Norvell said. "Threw the ball well. There were a couple of plays we're going to continue to learn from. (But) I thought, all in all, it was a good day on his behalf."

Good thing for the Tigers he likes to learn. The California native, who earned his undergraduate degree from Arizona State in less than three years and received his master's degree in sports commerce in August, said Saturday he is now pursuing a doctorate.

"It's a doctorate in liberal studies, but I get to pick my major concentrations and work with the faculty to kind of plan out my own road," White said. "The plan was to do a second master's. I was kind of thinking about doing the doctorate thing, but I thought it would be a little difficult to get into right away. But when I saw that option was available, I jumped on it. Absolutely, let's roll."

OPPOSITE: Memphis quarterback Brady White throws the ball against Southern during their game at Liberty Bowl Memorial Stadium on Sept. 7, 2019. JOE RONDONE / THE COMMERCIAL APPEAL

RIGHT: Memphis Mighty Sound of the South plays before the game against Southern. JOE RONDONE / THE COMMERCIAL APPEAL

OPPOSITE: Memphis running back Rodrigues Clark runs the ball against Southern. JOE RONDONE / THE COMMERCIAL APPEAL

BELOW RIGHT: Memphis linebacker Austin Hall celebrates a tackle in the backfield. JOE RONDONE / THE COMMERCIAL APPEAL

BELOW: Memphis running back Kenneth Gainwell leans forward for extra yards on a run against Southern. JOE RONDONE / THE COMMERCIAL APPEAL

LEFT: Memphis running back Timothy Taylor tries to juke past Southern cornerback Datrel Brumfield. JOE RONDONE / THE COMMERCIAL APPEAL

OPPOSITE: Memphis tight end Joey Magnifico catches a pass over the defense of Montavius Gaines of Southern. JOE RONDONE / THE COMMERCIAL APPEAL

BELOW LEFT: Memphis wide receiver Damonte Coxie tries to catch the ball against Southern defender O.J. Tucker. JOE RONDONE / THE COMMERCIAL APPEAL

Sports

MEMPHIS 55, SOUTHERN 24

Memphis running back Kenneth Gainwell takes it in for a 46-yard touchdown run against Southern on Saturday. JOE RONDONE/THE COMMERCIAL APPEAL

Don't worry just yet

Memphis shakes off slow start to take care of Southern

Damonte Coxie was lying on the turf in pain. Patrick Taylor was on crutches on the sideline. The Memphis football offense was averaging 2.6 yards per rush. The Memphis defense was catching its breath after allowing a 17-play touchdown drive that spanned more than 10 minutes of game action.

Two star players hurt less than two games into the 2019 football season. One SWAC team giving the Tigers more trouble than the SEC team they faced a week ago. And a question that could have crept into anyone's mind in that

Mark Giannotto
Columnist
Memphis Commercial Appeal
USA TODAY NETWORK – TENN.

moment: Should we be worried? Maybe not yet.

Not after the Tigers pulled away from Southern for a 55-24 win Saturday at Liberty Bowl Memorial Stadium.

Not after Coxie returned to the game and finished with six catches for 112

yards.

Not after quarterback Brady White looked better throwing the ball than at any point during his time as the starter here.

Not after redshirt freshman Kenneth Gainwell, on the very next play after Coxie was briefly left the game in the second quarter, burst through the line of scrimmage like he was shot out of a cannon for a 46-yard touchdown run.

See GIANNOTTO, Page 7B

What we learned from Tigers' win vs. Southern

Evan Barnes
Memphis Commercial Appeal
USA TODAY NETWORK – TENNESSEE

Midway through the third quarter against Memphis, Southern's band tried to will its team back at the Liberty Bowl.

After Jordan Lewis scored on a 74-yard fumble return to cut Memphis' lead to 10, the band played Lenny Kravitz's hit "It Ain't Over Til It's Over."

Memphis scored on its next three drives and was never threatened again in a 55-24 win Saturday when the Tigers' offense shined with 575 total yards.

Here's five takeaways from the Tigers improving to 2-0.

Have a day, Kenneth Gainwell

With Patrick Taylor out with injury, Gainwell assumed the bulk of the work and he didn't disappoint. The redshirt freshman had a game-high 16 carries, ran for two scores, including one for 46 yards, and caught a 21-yard touchdown pass

Gainwell finished with 123 all-purpose yards, including 85 rushing.

The Tigers offense was efficient

After a tough showing against Ole Miss, the Memphis passing game got back on track. Brady White (17-of-21, 337 yards, two touchdowns) looked his best as he challenged the Southern secondary downfield.

Damonte Coxie (six catches, 112 yards) had his first 100-yard receiving day of the season. Kedarian Jones had a 65-yard catch that set up Gainwell's second touchdown run. But the best highlight? Antonio Gibson's 55-yard touchdown catch where he shook off several would-be tacklers and fought his way to the end zone

Welcome back, Keith Brown

Brown hadn't played since suffering a season-ending injury nearly a year

See MEMPHIS, Page 7B

Henderson makes impact in MUS' win over Christian Brothers

Khari Thompson
Memphis Commercial Appeal
USA TODAY NETWORK – TENNESSEE

The first glimpse of MUS' Marcus Henderson during region play revealed a quicker, more durable version with stronger endurance.

The four-star 6-foot-5 lineman, who

year he only played offense. He played MUS' whole 37-24 win over rival Christian Brothers on both sides of the ball Friday.

"I'm just more versatile. I can play defense. I'm running around, having fun. Just being able to move quicker and faster," Henderson said.

Henderson posted 3.5 tackles in

1-0 DII-AAA West) in the victory over Christian Brothers (2-1, 0-1). He also helped pave the way for the MUS offense, which gained 259 yards and had four touchdowns.

"He wouldn't have been able to make as many plays as he made tonight last year," MUS coach Bobby Alston said.

one mile before his weightlifting sessions and one mile after.

"I was just eating fish and I was just having green leafy vegetables and drinking protein shakes. And then I was just drinking a whole lot of water, like that's pretty much all I was putting in my body. And lots of fruits, too," Hen-

Memphis ground game surges past South Alabama

BY EVAN BARNES • THE COMMERCIAL APPEAL

Kenneth Gainwell and Kylan Watkins don't have a rivalry. But when the Memphis running backs see each other make a play, it motivates them to top it.

"It's like a competition. If Kenny gets one, I know I got to bring it, too," Watkins said after the Tigers' 42-6 win over South Alabama, which was highlighted by both running backs having long runs that showed their speed.

Gainwell went first with a 71-yard run in the first quarter where the freshman burst from the left side and ran into open space before being pushed out of bounds at the South Alabama 11.

Watkins topped that in the second quarter with a 72-yard run. Both runs set up touchdowns by the Tigers and were highlights of each back having his first career 100-plus rushing yard day.

In Watkins' mind, his favorite play against the Jaguars wasn't a run. It was the sophomore's lone catch where he fully extended his body for an 18-yard touchdown from Brady White.

"I probably liked the catch more because the run, I got a little tired," Watkins said. "I really should've scored but I got a little fatigued on that play."

It added to a breakout game for the Whitehaven High School graduate. He had 113 rushing yards to complement Gainwell's 145.

After spring practice, coach Mike Norvell was high on the idea of Watkins having an impact this season. Now, with Patrick Taylor still out with an injury, Watkins added to form a formidable 1-2 running back punch as Memphis ran for a season-high 312 yards.

"You watched some of the early runs that he had and he was a little hesitant," Norvell said. "But as he got going and really in the rhythm of the game, I think the touchdown catch really gave him a springboard moving forward."

But are Gainwell and Watkins the new two-headed monster? It's too soon to tell if they inherited the nickname that Darrell Henderson gave himself and Taylor last season as the lead running backs.

OPPOSITE: Memphis running back Kenneth Gainwell escapes a diving Tré Young during a 71-yard run against South Alabama during their game at the Ladd-Peebles Stadium in Mobile, Alabama, on Sept. 14, 2019. JOE RONDONE / THE COMMERCIAL APPEAL

ABOVE: Memphis quarterback Connor Adair throws the ball after coming in to replace Brady White late in the win over South Alabama. JOE RONDONE / THE COMMERCIAL APPEAL

ABOVE LEFT: Memphis running back Kylan Watkins takes off for a 72-yard run. JOE RONDONE / THE COMMERCIAL APPEAL

OPPOSITE: Memphis Tigers head coach Mike Norvell prepares to lead his team out on to the field to take on the South Alabama Jaguars. JOE RONDONE / THE COMMERCIAL APPEAL

LEFT: Memphis running back Kenneth Gainwell takes off from the backfield. JOE RONDONE / THE COMMERCIAL APPEAL

RIGHT: Memphis linebacker Austin Hall returns a fumble for a touchdown against South Alabama. JOE RONDONE / THE COMMERCIAL APPEAL

OPPOSITE: Memphis defensive end Corteze Love celebrates with teammates after their 42-6 win over South Alabama. JOE RONDONE / THE COMMERCIAL APPEAL

BELOW RIGHT: Memphis players celebrate with Austin Hall, right, after his fumble recovery return for a touchdown against South Alabama. JOE RONDONE / THE COMMERCIAL APPEAL

Tigers storm back to sink Navy

BY EVAN BARNES • THE COMMERCIAL APPEAL

A 13-point deficit in the second quarter. Boo birds raining down at the Liberty Bowl. Everything looked bleak for Memphis football during this Thursday-night game.

Until it didn't.

Memphis rallied to prevail 35-23 over Navy as the offense found second life, special teams delivered and the Tigers' defense proved yet again why it might be the best unit coach Mike Norvell has had in his tenure.

Here's what we learned from Memphis improving to 4-0 (1-0 AAC) for the first time since 2015.

Kenneth Gainwell, Antonio Gibson show out

Another game, another big play for Gainwell. His latest highlight was a 75-yard rushing touchdown on the Tigers' first play from scrimmage. He became the third freshman in Memphis history to have multiple 100-yard rushing games, finishing with 104 rushing yards

But this was Gibson's breakthrough performance. Not only did the senior have a 73-yard touchdown catch in the third quarter, but he added 88 kickoff return yards and finished with a career-high 105 receiving yards.

Tigers' offense rallies in the second half

Brady White was the target of the boos to start the third quarter after he missed two open receivers by overthrowing out of bounds. The Tigers ended up settling for a three-and-out.

How did he respond? By throwing touchdown passes on Memphis' next three scoring drives to three different receivers. Kedarian Jones' 5-yard touchdown put the Tigers up for good and, after Gibson's long score, White threw a tight ball to Damonte Coxie on third down that ended up a 31-yard touchdown.

White had only 29 passing yards at halftime but finished with 196.

Memphis' defense bends but does not yield

Navy had 373 total yards thanks to its triple option, but the Tigers adjusted to limit the Midshipmen to only 81 after halftime.

Navy had success early rushing to the outside, and Keoni-Kordell Makekau became the first running back to go over 100 yards against the Tigers this season. But Memphis held Navy without a touchdown in the second half as Adam Fuller's unit once again proved it could withstand pressure and punch back.

OPPOSITE: Memphis Tigers players take the field to play Navy at Liberty Bowl Memorial Stadium on Sept. 26, 2019.
JOE RONDONE / THE COMMERCIAL APPEAL

ABOVE: Memphis Tigers wide receiver Damonte Coxie catches and runs in a 31-yard touchdown against Navy. JOE RONDONE / THE COMMERCIAL APPEAL

ABOVE RIGHT: Memphis Tigers linebacker Xavier Cullens drags down Navy running back CJ Williams. JOE RONDONE / THE COMMERCIAL APPEAL

OPPOSITE: Memphis Tigers wide receiver Kedarian Jones breaks past Navy safety Evan Fochtman. JOE RONDONE / THE COMMERCIAL APPEAL

RIGHT: Memphis Tigers defensive back Tyrez Lindsey tackles Navy quarterback Malcolm Perry. JOE RONDONE / THE COMMERCIAL APPEAL

Bad throw sparks turnaround for White

BY MARK GIANNOTTO • THE COMMERCIAL APPEAL

> "I just need to relax, execute, let the game come to me. Not try to force the issue and trust what I'm seeing."
>
> BRADY WHITE

It was the worst throw of his Memphis football career. It had to have been.

Quarterback Brady White stepped up in the pocket with room to run on the opening possession of the second half. He had one receiver streaking open down the seam. He had junior Damonte Coxie so wide open along the sideline there wasn't a defender within 10 yards. He had to get a first down. He had to do anything but what he ended up doing.

Because he ended up overthrowing Coxie so badly, the reaction was merciless. The 33,909 fans at Liberty Bowl Memorial Stadium booed. ESPN's Matt Hasselbeck called it "just an absolutely terrible throw" on the television broadcast.

Once White was sacked on the next play, social media lit up with people begging for coach Mike Norvell to make a quarterback change. Some even took victory laps pointing out how long ago they declared White's play to be insufficient.

But here's the part that should endear White to Memphis fans more than ever before. The part that led to a smile Norvell couldn't stop talking about after the game. The part that ultimately propelled the Tigers to a 35-23 win over Navy.

White had an answer for all those boo birds and critics and doubters.

He answered them with dinks and dunks and a short touchdown pass to wide receiver Kedarian Jones that gave Memphis the lead in a game it had no business leading at that point.

Then he answered them with perhaps the best throw of his Memphis football career. A 73-yard bomb to senior Antonio Gibson over the top of the Navy defense. On third-and-13, no less.

"I saw him smile," Norvell said about that one, "and when I saw him smile I knew it was on."

But then, in case anybody missed all that, White stepped up in the pocket again, worked through his progressions and saw Coxie open again. But he didn't miss again.

One 31-yard touchdown strike later, using the exact same play call as the Gibson touchdown before it, the Tigers suddenly looked like an undefeated team ready to go on a run this season.

"It was my favorite play," Norvell said.

So after the pass ridiculed around the country, after the boos rained down, White went 10 of 12 for 167 yards and two touchdowns.

It's hard to overemphasize how important all of this was, and not just because White was left for dead by just about everyone not wearing a black Memphis

Tigers uniform.

In the 17 games he started before, ever since White came to Memphis from Arizona State, he had never won a game with his arm.

He relied on the electricity of Darrell Henderson last year or, against Ole Miss earlier this month, a key stop from the defense. Each time White's arm entered the spotlight, the ball inevitably fell short.

That finally changed on an evening that will be remembered if this Memphis team eventually wins an American Athletic Conference title and gets to a New Year's Six bowl game.

White tersely said, "I don't care" when asked about the boos. He conceded that overthrow "was probably deserving of the crowd reaction." He noted his parents, who were in the stands along with his girlfriend and some family friends, "are more affected than me."

"I just need to do my dang job and execute," White said. "I just need to relax, execute, let the game come to me. Not try to force the issue and trust what I'm seeing."

But Norvell admitted he was worried, and he offered support not criticism on the sideline in that moment of crisis. It's a reminder of why White didn't deserve those boos, and not because they became

LEFT: Memphis Tigers quarterback Brady White throws past Navy striker Jacob Springer. JOE RONDONE / THE COMMERCIAL APPEAL

the catalyst for something special against Navy.

The polarizing opinions and skepticism concerning White's play are valid. But they're also the result of Norvell's unwavering confidence in him, a belief that ultimately led three quarterbacks to transfer elsewhere since White's arrival.

Who knows if White can back up Norvell's faith every time Memphis needs a play from its quarterback? But Thursday night, he rewarded his coach with a smile.

"When I saw him smile, I knew it was on," Norvell repeated. "That guy is pretty dang special."

ABOVE: Memphis Tigers celebrate during the game against the Navy Midshipmen. JUSTIN FORD / USA TODAY SPORTS

ABOVE RIGHT: Memphis Tigers defensive lineman Morris Joseph celebrates a sack against Navy. JOE RONDONE / THE COMMERCIAL APPEAL

OPPOSITE: Memphis Tigers wide receiver Damonte Coxie celebrates with his teammates after their 35-23 win over Navy. JOE RONDONE / THE COMMERCIAL APPEAL

RIGHT: Memphis Tigers wide receiver Damonte Coxie looks back at Navy defender Jacob Springer as he runs in a 31-yard touchdown. JOE RONDONE / THE COMMERCIAL APPEAL

Tigers gather themselves to finish strong

BY EVAN BARNES • THE COMMERCIAL APPEAL

MONROE, La. - It was a sense of déjà vu for Memphis. A fourth-quarter lead that slowly was wilting in the Bayou heat.

But the Tigers turned to two things that had defined their season. First Kenneth Gainwell burst free for a 68-yard touchdown. Then La'Andre Thomas sealed the 52-33 victory with an interception return for a touchdown.

On a day where Memphis had its toughest road test, the Tigers survived to improve to 5-0. Here's what we learned at Malone Stadium:

Kenneth Gainwell makes history

Gainwell did not start the game as he was dealing with a lower leg injury, according to the ESPN broadcast. It didn't matter as he became the first Memphis freshman running back with three consecutive 100-yard games.

Gainwell scored twice and finished with 209 rushing yards, the most ever by a Memphis freshman running back. The previous record was 206 by Larry Porter in 1990 against Arkansas State.

Memphis added some trickery in the first half when Riley Patterson recovered his onside kick after the Tigers scored a touchdown. After Memphis scored on a 14-yard catch by Kylan Watkins, holder Preston Brady took the snap and ran in the two-point conversion, Memphis' first since 2016.

Offensive lineman Scottie Dill added a blocked field goal right before halftime, the Tigers' third blocked kick of the season. Adam Williams had a career-high 77-yard punt and Patterson added a 50-yard field goal, his second career make of 50 or more yards.

Defense struggles with rushing game

The Tigers once again struggled with a mobile quarterback, as ULM's Caleb Evans broke his share of tackles and escaped for extra yards. When Evans escaped to throw, he often found open receivers against a Tigers' unit that ranked No. 1 in passing yards allowed per game prior to this contest.

It was far from Memphis' finest hour as missed tackles led to Evans and Josh Johnson rushing for over 100 yards each. ULM had 575 total yards, outgaining Memphis by 40.

Brady White was mostly sharp

White was efficient in the first half with only two incompletions and showed his toughness in the pocket on a 15-yard pass to Kedarian Jones while being hit. The second half was more of a struggle, underscored by White throwing an interception in the fourth quarter.

He finished with 249 passing yards on 15-of-23 passing and threw three touchdown passes for the third consecutive game. But with the offense stalling in the

---

OPPOSITE: Memphis wide receiver Antonio Gibson cuts past University of Louisiana-Monroe safety Austin Hawley at Malone Stadium in Monroe, Louisiana, on Oct. 5, 2019. JOE RONDONE / THE COMMERCIAL APPEAL

second half, it was not a complete performance from the Tigers' quarterback.

Memphis still has not played a complete game

The Tigers might be a Top 25 team in the Amway Coaches Poll at No. 23 and off to their best start in four years, but they have yet to look like it for four quarters.

ULM's second-half play gave fans flashbacks of last year when Memphis let fourth-quarter leads slip away. It was a reminder they couldn't afford any lapses if they want to contend for an AAC championship.

ABOVE RIGHT: Memphis quarterback Brady White hands off to running back Kenneth Gainwell. JOE RONDONE / THE COMMERCIAL APPEAL

FAR RIGHT: Memphis linebacker Austin Hall tackles ULM's Zach Jackson. JOE RONDONE / THE COMMERCIAL APPEAL

RIGHT: Memphis quarterback Brady White throws a touchdown pass to Damonte Coxie. JOE RONDONE / THE COMMERCIAL APPEAL

Sports

Assessing Tigers after a 5-0 start

Memphis cornerback Carlito Gonzalez jars the ball loose on a hit against ULM wide receiver Will Derrick on Saturday.
JOE RONDONE/THE COMMERCIAL APPEAL

Ugly win proves there is room for improvement

Evan Barnes
Memphis Commercial Appeal
USA TODAY NETWORK – TENNESSEE

MONROE, La. — It wasn't the prettiest Memphis football win of the year. In fact, it was probably the ugliest.

The Tigers were outgained by Louisiana-Monroe. They lost the turnover battle thanks to a Brady White interception and a fumble by Joey Magnifico.

Tigers survive game and move to 5-0 season start

Evan Barnes
Memphis Commercial Appeal
USA TODAY NETWORK – TENNESSEE

MONROE, La. — It was a sense of déjà vu for Memphis. A fourth-quarter lead that slowly was wilting in the Bayou heat.

But the Tigers turned to two things that have defined its season. First Kenneth Gainwell burst free for a 60-yard touchdown. Then La'Andre Thomas

3 things from Grizzlies preseason opener

David Cobb
Memphis Commercial Appeal
USA TODAY NETWORK – TENNESSEE

Ja Morant flew in between three defenders for an offensive rebound and dribbled toward the corner.

Then he turned around and fired a pass between the same three defenders to a cutting Dillon Brooks, who finished a layup.

As Morant ran back down the court after his third quarter rebound-assist combo, he circled his fingers around his eyes to mimic a pair of binoculars.

Morant scored 10 points in the Grizzlies' 123-88 preseason opening win over Israeli professional team Maccabi Haifa on Sunday at FedExForum.

More importantly, he showed the athleticism and awareness – sometimes both in the same play – that made him the No. 2 pick in June's draft as the Grizzlies began their preseason slate with an easy victory.

Ja Morant's debut

Morant took his man off the dribble to the baseline for a layup on the game's first possession. He followed that up with a turnover.

Such is life with a rookie point guard.

But by the time he checked out for good after playing 19 minutes, the encouraging plays outweighed the bad for Morant.

"I thought he did a pretty good job there weaving himself into the paint and making the unselfish plays," coach Taylor Jenkins said.

At one point late in the first quarter, Morant made a backdoor cut and threw down a vicious dunk.

He blew by a defender for a left-handed layup soon after that.

Morant made five of eight attempts from the field, missing his only 3-point try. He also dished out seven assists.

"I had to be strong, not try to get emotional or anything," Morant said. "The first NBA game, even though it's preseason, it's still a wild moment at the end of the day."

Playing small

With starting center Jonas Valanciunas out because of foot soreness,

ABOVE: Memphis running back Kenneth Gainwell celebrates on the field during the Tigers 52-33 win.

JOE RONDONE / THE COMMERCIAL APPEAL

LEFT: Memphis quarterback Brady White celebrates with fans after their win against ULM. JOE RONDONE / THE COMMERCIAL APPEAL

OPPOSITE: Memphis head coach Mike Norvell talks to his team during a timeout. JOE RONDONE / THE COMMERCIAL APPEAL

BELOW LEFT: Memphis running back Kenneth Gainwell takes off out of the backfield. JOE RONDONE / THE COMMERCIAL APPEAL

BELOW: Memphis wide receiver Damonte Coxie celebrates his touchdown with Kedarian Jones. JOE RONDONE / THE COMMERCIAL APPEAL

Tigers fight, but Temple wins the battle

BY EVAN BARNES • THE COMMERCIAL APPEAL

In a city known for its boxing heroes, Memphis showed more than enough fight after trailing by 16.

Despite four turnovers, the Tigers clawed their way back and marched down in Temple territory with under three minutes left. Then a fourth-down pass to Joey Magnifico was ruled incomplete, sending Temple into wild celebration.

Memphis' perfect start came to an end with a 30-28 loss at Lincoln Financial Field. Here's what we learned:

The first quarter? A disaster

It was the worst possible start for Memphis (5-1, 1-1) to resume AAC play. A poor Brady White throw was tossed into the hands of a Temple defender, and on the Tigers' next two possessions, White also played a role in two fumbles after a strip sack and a fumbled exchange.

The Memphis defense held Temple (5-1, 1-1) to field goals after each turnover, but Memphis played as poorly as one could against a defense ranked in the top 20 nationally in four categories entering this game.

Good day, bad day for Brady White

White threw for a career-high 363 yards, but he had a hand in all four turnovers by the offense. Memphis trailed 16-0 thanks to the turnovers, and White's fumble to open the fourth quarter was a costly mistake that Temple turned into a scoring drive.

The bright side was White helped the Tigers fight back by leading the offense on two scoring drives just before halftime. Damonte Coxie had 92 yards on eight catches, and Magnifico added a career-high 87 receiving yards.

Another big game for Kenneth Gainwell

It's getting more obvious each week, but Gainwell's star keeps growing brighter. He had a career-high eight receptions for 98 yards.

He also ran for 106 yards, extending his Memphis record for most consecutive 100-yard rushing games by a freshman and tying DeAngelo Williams' record for most total 100-yard rushing games by a Memphis freshman.

Memphis defense gets stops but not enough

Memphis again turned to its defense to bail it out and nearly pulled it off. The Tigers held Temple to field goals after that three-turnover mess in the first, and Joseph Dorceus recovered a fumble in the second that led to a Memphis scoring drive.

T.J. Carter added a strip as Temple was driving in the red zone in the third quarter. Austin Hall added a crucial fourth-down stop with 5:20 left, but the Tigers' defense also gave up a late touchdown pass after White's fumble that proved to be just enough to keep the Owls ahead.

OPPOSITE: Memphis Tigers running back Kylan Watkins drags Temple Owls defender Chapelle Russell into the end zone for a touchdown during their game at Lincoln Financial Field in Philadelphia on Oct. 12, 2019. JOE RONDONE / THE COMMERCIAL APPEAL

ABOVE: Memphis Tigers running back Kenneth Gainwell breaks downfield. JOE RONDONE / THE COMMERCIAL APPEAL

ABOVE RIGHT: Memphis Tigers wide receiver Kedarian Jones makes a sideline catch. JOE RONDONE / THE COMMERCIAL APPEAL

OPPOSITE: Memphis Tigers running back Kenneth Gainwell breaks up the field. JOE RONDONE / THE COMMERCIAL APPEAL

RIGHT: Memphis Tigers running back Kenneth Gainwell shakes off Temple Owls defenders, including cornerback Harrison Hand (23), for a touchdown. JOE RONDONE / THE COMMERCIAL APPEAL

Catch or not? Call spoils Tigers' perfect season

BY MARK GIANNOTTO • THE COMMERCIAL APPEAL

They thought it was a catch.

Coach Mike Norvell. Tight end Joey Magnifico. Cornerback T.J. Carter. Running back Kenneth Gainwell. Quarterback Brady White.

They all thought it was a catch.

"Everybody on the sideline thought it was a catch," Magnifico said.

Everybody, as it turned out, except the replay official at Lincoln Financial Field. And it's all anybody wanted to talk about after Memphis suffered a 30-28 loss at Temple.

So let's go right to that moment. Right past the three first-quarter turnovers by White and right past the 16-0 hole Memphis almost climbed out from. Right past the fourth White turnover that shifted momentum back to Temple again. Right past the biggest reasons the Tigers lost this game.

It's fourth-and-7 with less than two minutes to go and a Temple defender is grabbing the "White" on the back of White's jersey. So he just heaves the ball downfield in the general direction of Magnifico.

The ball sails through the air for seemingly forever as Magnifico sprints and dives to reach it. For about a minute, the goat is the hero. For about a minute, the end to the Tigers' comeback is finally in sight.

For about a minute, the replay official is reviewing the play. And everyone in this cavernous NFL stadium, and everyone watching at home, is trying to watch what he's watching.

"I know there was movement within the ball, but it's a pretty big jumbotron," Norvell said. "It looked like his arm was underneath it."

"I knew it was a catch," Magnifico said. "I caught it 100 percent."

But after about a minute elapsed, an official came to the Memphis huddle to tell the Tigers that the play had been reversed. That the ball hit the ground. That it wasn't a catch. That, in effect, Memphis won't improve to 6-0 for just the third time in program history.

The American Athletic Conference did not make the replay official available for comment because it was a judgment call, citing a league policy.

"The ruling was that the Memphis player didn't have control of the ball as it hit the ground and that there was enough video evidence to confirm it," AAC assistant commissioner Chuck Sullivan told a pool reporter.

Did the ball hit the ground? Maybe. But nothing from the replays shown on television equaled indisputable video evidence to reverse the call on the field of a catch.

"I guess they had a more conclusive angle to decide that it needed to be overturned," Norvell said. "But from my vantage point on the jumbotron, it looked like it was a catch."

Here's what can't be disputed, though: The Tigers aren't good enough to turn the ball over four times and win a road game.

Their defense, while improved, isn't good enough to be on the field for 20 minutes in the first half. Their quarterback isn't good enough to overcome three fumbles and a terrible interception that ultimately led to 16 Temple points.

The telling moment came just as Memphis was in the middle of grabbing momentum back after a disastrous first quarter.

As running back Kenneth Gainwell crossed the goal line in the second quarter, ESPN play-by-play announcer Anish Shroff told the entire country what Temple's coaches told him before Saturday's game.

"If Memphis is going to beat us," Shroff said, "it's going to be Brady White throwing downfield."

Well, White threw for more yards than he's ever thrown for before (373). And he did help Memphis beat someone. The only problem, of course, is that the Tigers beat themselves.

Which made this especially painful.

> ## "I knew it was a catch. I caught it 100 percent."
> JOEY MAGNIFICO

But in proving they're imperfect, the Tigers also proved something else.

They're still good enough to win the AAC West. They're still good enough to achieve every goal they set out to achieve this season.

Just look at how this game unfolded.

Temple couldn't land the knockout blow when it had the chance.

It couldn't get more than three field goals courtesy of Memphis' disastrous first quarter. A first quarter that featured a terrible interception by White, a terrible fumble by White and a terrible fumbled exchange. The Tigers were teetering.

"That was embarrassing. I need to get better," White said. "You can't have those."

And then, in the city where Rocky Balboa came to life, the Tigers got off the mat.

Suddenly, a 16-point deficit had turned into a nail-biter. Temple 23, Memphis 21, and plenty of time to go.

Plenty of time, it turned out, to fall just short.

ABOVE: Memphis Tigers wide receiver Damonte Coxie stares down a Temple Owls defender after catching a pass. JOE RONDONE / THE COMMERCIAL APPEAL

OPPOSITE: Memphis Tigers quarterback Brady White walks off the field after their 30-28 loss to the Temple Owls. JOE RONDONE / THE COMMERCIAL APPEAL

Sports

TEMPLE 30, MEMPHIS 28

What we learned from Tigers' loss at Temple

Evan Barnes Memphis Commercial Appeal
USA TODAY NETWORK – TENNESSEE

PHILADELPHIA — In a city known for its boxing heroes, Memphis showed more than enough fight after trailing by 16.

Despite four turnovers, the Tigers clawed their way back and marched down in Temple territory with under three minutes left. Then a fourth-down pass to Joey Magnifico was ruled incomplete, sending Temple into wild celebration.

Memphis' perfect start came to an end with a 30-28 loss at Lincoln Financial Field. Here's what we learned Saturday.

The first quarter? A disaster

It was the worst possible start for Memphis (5-1, 1-1) to resume AAC play.

A poor Brady White throw was tossed into the hands of a Temple (5-1, 1-1) defender, and on the Tigers' next two possessions, White also played a role in two fumbles after a strip sack and a fumbled exchange.

See TIGERS, Page 6B

Memphis Tigers quarterback Brady White throws a pass while being hit by Temple Owls defender Quincy Roche on Saturday. JOE RONDONE/THE COMMERCIAL APPEAL

Call costs Memphis chance to win, not reason Tigers lost

Mark Giannotto
Columnist
Memphis Commercial Appeal
USA TODAY NETWORK – TENN.

PHILADELPHIA — They thought it was a catch. Coach Mike Norvell. Tight end Joey Magnifico. Cornerback T.J. Carter. Running back Kenneth Gainwell. Quarterback Brady White.

They all thought it was a catch.

"Everybody on the sideline thought it was a catch," Magnifico said.

Everybody, as it turned out, except the replay official at Lincoln Financial Field Saturday afternoon. And it's all anybody wanted to talk about after Memphis suffered a 30-28 loss at Temple.

So let's go right to that moment. Right past the three first-quarter turnovers by White and right past the 16-0 hole Memphis almost climbed out from. Right past the fourth White turnover that shifted momentum back to Temple again. Right past the biggest reasons the Tigers lost this game.

It's fourth-and-7 with less than two minutes to go and a Temple defender is grabbing the "White" on the back of White's jersey. So he just heaves the ball downfield in the general direction of Magnifico.

The ball sails through the air for seemingly forever as Magnifico sprints and dives to reach it. For about a minute, the goat is the hero. For about a minute, the end to the Tigers' comeback is finally in sight.

For about a minute, the replay official is reviewing the play. And everyone in this cavernous NFL

See GIANNOTTO, Page 6B

Tigers vs. The World

BY JASON MUNZ • THE COMMERCIAL APPEAL

"Sometimes it really is Memphis vs. everybody."

Dialing up the sentiment that has become ubiquitous with the Memphis sports scene in recent years — albeit slightly paraphrasing the original, "Memphis vs. Errbody" — university President Dr. M. David Rudd took to Twitter in the moments after last week's controversial loss at Temple and reignited the movement.

The Tigers put that us-against-the-world mentality on display in the buildup to and during their 47-17 beatdown of Tulane. The university decided shortly after the previous week's letdown to promote the "Memphis vs. Everybody" theme for the team's return to Liberty Bowl Memorial Stadium after the Temple loss.

It worked.

Memphis blasted the Green Wave, avenging a 40-24 loss in New Orleans a season ago, on the strength of more than 300 yards of total offense from Kenneth Gainwell. As fast as the redshirt freshman's star continues to rise, it was fitting the Tigers benefited from a bounty of standout performances from a handful players from Memphis and the surrounding area.

Joey Magnifico, a senior from Cordova, caught three balls for 31 yards and a touchdown. Austin Hall, a senior from Collierville, had an interception, a pass breakup and three tackles (including 1.5 for loss). Thomas Pickens, a redshirt junior who attended Memphis University School, also snagged an interception and finished with five tackles. Calvin Austin III, a redshirt sophomore who graduated from Harding Academy in Memphis, caught two passes — both touchdowns (the first two of his Tigers career).

The significance of their performances, on "Memphis vs. Everybody" Night, was not lost on coach Mike Norvell.

"I love that mind-set," he said. "We've got something special here. We've got a special community. We've got a special brand we represent. You get an opportunity to step on that field, there's only one way to do it.

"It was a great night for Memphis."

Whether this game was billed as "Memphis vs. Everybody" or not, it didn't matter to the Tigers, according to Pickens.

"That theme (is) every time we play in the Liberty Bowl," he said. "Every time we put on the jersey. I mean, that's just the theme every game, every practice, everything we do."

Magnifico, who said he left all the controversy that followed the catch he made on fourth-and-long against Temple — a catch that was eventually overturned — agreed with Pickens.

"That's just how it is around here," he said. "When you come to Memphis, you might not start off liking it, but the culture changes you. By the end of the time you're here, you're going to be a Memphian, for real."

OPPOSITE: Memphis players run out on to the field for their game against Tulane at Liberty Bowl Memorial Stadium on Oct. 19, 2019.
JOE RONDONE / THE COMMERCIAL APPEAL

Memphis running back Kenneth Gainwell is pinned between Tulane defenders Thakarius Keyes, left, and Patrick Johnson.

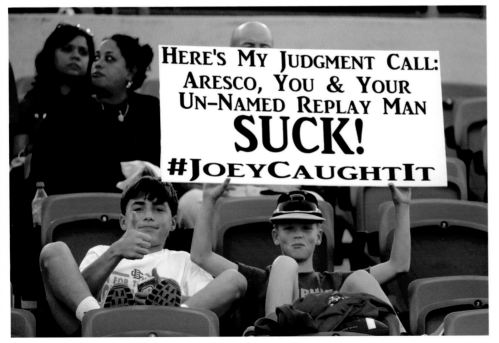

ABOVE: Memphis tight end Joey Magnifico breaks into the end zone for a touchdown against Tulane. JOE RONDONE / THE COMMERCIAL APPEAL

ABOVE LEFT: Memphis' Chris Claybrooks returns a kickoff. JOE RONDONE / THE COMMERCIAL APPEAL

LEFT: Fans watch as Memphis takes on Tulane. JOE RONDONE / THE COMMERCIAL APPEAL

ABOVE: Memphis defenders Austin Hall, left, and T.J. Carter combine to tackle Tulane wide receiver Jalen McCleskey. JOE RONDONE / THE COMMERCIAL APPEAL

ABOVE RIGHT: Memphis running back Kenneth Gainwell tries to stiff arm his way past Tulane defender Chase Kuerschen. JOE RONDONE / THE COMMERCIAL APPEAL

RIGHT: Memphis running back Kenneth Gainwell celebrates a touchdown against Tulane. JOE RONDONE / THE COMMERCIAL APPEAL

Sports

Inside

▌AAC championship game will stay as is thanks to NCAA waiver grant. **2B**

Memphis running back Kenneth Gainwell celebrates his touchdown with Kedarian Jones against Tulane during their game at the Liberty Bowl Memorial Stadium on Saturday. JOE RONDONE/THE COMMERCIAL APPEAL

Memphis makes a big statement

Mark Giannotto
Columnist
Memphis Commercial Appeal
USA TODAY NETWORK – TENN.

They stood up ready to riot. The Memphis fans in "Memphis

der review," referee Charles Lamertina said over the public address system at Liberty Bowl Memorial Stadium.

The boos arrived almost instantaneously. This catch, a 12-yard reception for a first down by wide receiver Damonte Coxie, wasn't nearly as consequential as last week

blame them?

"The call stands," Lamertina announced after the short review.

He sounded relieved. Like he knew what he was up against. Like a man who knew he had to walk out of this stadium at some point Saturday night.

Tigers' Gainwell in awe of his stats

Evan Barnes
Memphis Commercial Appeal
USA TODAY NETWORK – TENNESSEE

Memphis coach Mike Norvell took his time reading the stat sheet after the Tigers' 47-17 win over Tulane. His eyes lit up when he realized what Kenneth Gainwell did Saturday.

Moments later, Gainwell walked in and sat down. Norvell just laughed at the latest accomplishment by his running back.

"Good job tonight," Norvell said to Gainwell.

The freshman's latest performance was his best in a season where he continues to top himself.

After a week where he was named to the Associated Press and Sporting News midseason All-American teams, Gainwell became the first NCAA player since Louisiana Tech's Troy Edwards in 1997 to have 200 receiving yards and 100 rushing yards in the same game.

His career-best 203 receiving yards on a career-high nine catches made him the second Memphis player to have 200 receiving yards after Anthony Miller. He added 104 rushing yards, which made him the first Tigers freshman with five 100-yard rushing games.

"I'm just shocked right now," said Gainwell, who also had three total touchdowns. "I'm just blessed to come to work every day. I just try to make sure

See GAINWELL, Page 2B

Grizzlies' depth chart looks set

David Cobb
Memphis Commercial Appeal
USA TODAY NETWORK – TENNESSEE

Solomon Hill said before Grizzlies training camp began that the way to stay prepared for life in the NBA is to

Tigers catch a break

BY EVAN BARNES • THE COMMERCIAL APPEAL

TULSA, Okla. - It looked like a good sign for Memphis when one of Tulsa's flagbearers stumbled after leading the team out during pregame.

The fall proved a foreshadowing for the Tigers. Ahead by one, Memphis had to agonize as Tulsa set up for a 29-yard field goal with two seconds remaining.

Brady White and Antonio Gibson were among the players who said prayers on the sidelines. When Jacob Rainey's attempt went wide left, the Tigers stormed the field as they survived a 42-41 win at H.A. Chapman Stadium.

Several Memphis assistants pounded the wall of their coaches' box and yelled "Let's Go!" as they ran down to the field. A 14-point second-quarter lead evaporating didn't matter as the Tigers (7-1, 3-1) once again showed resiliency that has defined their season.

Here's what we learned:

Brady White delivers late

White's second half against Tulsa (2-6, 0-4) didn't match the brilliance of his first, but he was on time with a 57-yard pass to a wide-open Damonte Coxie on the Tigers' final scoring drive.

The Memphis offense was mostly stifled in the second half with only 179 yards, but White's throw and Coxie's run after the catch was as clutch a play as the Tigers had all season. White finished 15 of 25 with 277 yards and Coxie had 112 receiving yards on five catches.

Kenneth Gainwell shines despite a rare mistake

Gainwell had his sixth consecutive 100-yard game (149 rushing yards and three touchdowns), the third-longest streak in Tigers history. But the freshman had a fourth-quarter fumble that led to a Tulsa field goal.

He made up for it with a 1-yard touchdown that put Memphis back in the lead with 4:26 left. Gainwell finished with a career-high 24 carries to shoulder the Tigers' load once again.

The Tigers defense had a troubling performance

Tulsa entered ranked 10th in the AAC in passing offense and Memphis was tied for ninth nationally in pass defense. But Tulsa gashed the Tigers for big plays through the air.

The culprit for Memphis' struggles? Tulsa finished 14-for-24 on third- and fourth-down conversions. It also didn't help that the Tigers allowed Tulsa to go on consecutive five-minute scoring drives in the second half to take the lead.

It was the worst possible time for a bad showing. Tulsa finished with 584 total yards of offense, the most Memphis has allowed all season.

Memphis' usually reliable special teams were uneven

Quindell Johnson blocked a field goal and the Tigers pulled off trickery on a fake punt where Adam Williams threw a 29-yard pass to Calvin Austin III. But there were uncharacteristic mistakes.

Williams shanked a 21-yard punt in the first half. Riley Patterson missed a 33-yard field goal just before halftime and Chris Claybrooks had a fumble on a kickoff return. It just added to the mistakes that the Tigers had on the road.

OPPOSITE: Memphis Tigers wide receiver Calvin Austin III (84) leaps for a catch against the Tulsa Golden Hurricane during the first quarter at Skelly Field at H.A. Chapman Stadium on Oct. 26, 2019. ALONZO ADAMS / USA TODAY SPORTS

RIGHT: Memphis Tigers quarterback Brady White passes the ball to Memphis Tigers running back Kylan Watkins. ALONZO ADAMS / USA TODAY SPORTS

OPPOSITE: Tigers running back Kenneth Gainwell runs for a touchdown ahead of Tulsa Golden Hurricane safety Cristian Williams. ALONZO ADAMS / USA TODAY SPORTS

BELOW RIGHT: Tigers running back Kylan Watkins reaches but cannot catch a pass during a play against the Tulsa Golden Hurricane. ALONZO ADAMS / USA TODAY SPORTS

BELOW: Tigers wide receiver Calvin Austin III makes a catch on a fourth down pass as Tulsa Golden Hurricane cornerback Reggie Robinson II defends. ALONZO ADAMS / USA TODAY SPORTS

'We were going to give everything we had to the end'

BY EVAN BARNES • THE COMMERCIAL APPEAL

TULSA, Okla. - Mike Norvell sat to catch his breath. Brady White and Antonio Gibson shared a hug below H.A. Chapman Stadium

In the aftermath of the No. 25 Tigers' 42-41 thrilling win at Tulsa Saturday, the quiet was necessary. As support personnel moved quickly to pack the team's gear, Memphis Tigers coach Norvell looked down, up and gathered himself after Gibson spoke to the media

Before Tulsa's Jacob Rainey missed a last-second field goal, Norvell saw the faces on his team. He knew they still had some fight even the odds look bleak when Rainey lined up from 29 yards.

"Those kids' eyes, they knew no matter what we were going to give everything we had to the end of this game," Norvell said.

Now Memphis goes from surviving another test to preparing for its biggest one of the season: an SMU team (8-0, 4-0) that comes to the Liberty Bowl motivated by its best start since 1982.

Not only are the Tigers a game behind No. 17 SMU in the AAC West standings, it will be only the second time in Memphis history that a ranked Tigers team will host a ranked opponent.

It also is a game where the winner could take a step ahead in the race for the Group of Five's New Year's Six bowl bid.

"For us to be the nationally-showcased game on ABC, what more could you ask for?" Norvell said. "The fact that our city, our team, this university is going to be on display to show the world and the country what we're all about. That's why we do what we do."

The Tigers have won five consecutive games against SMU, often in spectacular fashion. Paxton Lynch threw seven touchdowns in the first half against the Mustangs in 2015 and the Tigers scored 66 points on SMU two years ago.

This is a different Mustangs team. Thanks to graduate transfer quarterback Shane Buchele, SMU is 10th nationally in total offense. SMU's defense is also much improved with an AAC-leading 36 sacks this season

It's also a different Memphis team. One that's been battle tested and ready to expand on its 10-1 record in November since Norvell arrived before the 2016 season.

ABOVE: Memphis Tigers quarterback Brady White hands off the ball to running back Kenneth Gainwell. ALONZO ADAMS / USA TODAY SPORTS

OPPOSITE: Memphis Tigers wide receiver Kedarian Jones makes a catch against the Tulsa Golden Hurricane for a first down.
ALONZO ADAMS / USA TODAY SPORTS

ABOVE: Tulsa Golden Hurricane quarterback Zach Smith is tackled by Memphis Tigers defensive lineman Joseph Dorceus. ALONZO ADAMS / USA TODAY SPORTS

LEFT: Memphis Tigers running back Kenneth Gainwell runs in for a touchdown beside Tulsa Golden Hurricane safety Manny Bunch. ALONZO ADAMS / USA TODAY SPORTS

OPPOSITE: The Memphis Tigers tackle Tulsa Golden Hurricane running back Corey Taylor II. ALONZO ADAMS / USA TODAY SPORTS

ABOVE LEFT: The Memphis Tigers celebrate after defeating the Tulsa Golden Hurricane 42-41 following a game-ending missed field goal. ALONZO ADAMS / USA TODAY SPORTS

OPPOSITE: Memphis Tigers running back Kenneth Gainwell celebrates after a touchdown against the Tulsa Golden Hurricane. ALONZO ADAMS / USA TODAY SPORTS

BELOW LEFT: Memphis Tigers defensive back La'Andre Thomas tackles Tulsa Golden Hurricane wide receiver Sam Crawford Jr. as Memphis Tigers defensive end Everitt Cunningham looks on. ALONZO ADAMS / USA TODAY SPORTS

A football celebration on Beale Street

BY MARK GIANNOTTO • THE COMMERCIAL APPEAL

MEMPHIS - Amanda McMinn was standing there with her poster board before Beale Street was completely and astoundingly full of people and signs and flags and just pure, unadulterated fun unlike anything Memphis has ever seen.

This was before Mike Norvell and Penny Hardaway appeared. Before Jerry "The King" Lawler showed up in a Batmobile and Lee Corso dressed up as Elvis for a perfectly executed heel turn. Before the sun had even come up.

"11th wedding anniversary and my husband brought me to College GameDay. #besthusbandever," McMinn had written on her sign.

Which is not actually the important part, even though McMinn described this particular anniversary as a "dream" for her and her husband, Mark, who owns Dyer's Burgers.

Because then she introduced her father. Freddie Veteto drove overnight from Destin, Florida, to be standing there on the corner of Beale and B.B. King Boulevard on this Saturday morning with his daughter and his grandson, Brayden.

Three generations of Memphis fans, scrunched along the sidewalk and street with thousands more just like them, marveling at the history they were witnessing.

"This is like dying and going to heaven," Veteto said. "Never thought the Tigers would get here."

Event surpasses the hype

This Saturday was about joy and satisfaction. The joy of being there for a once-in-a-lifetime moment in a one-of-a-kind setting, and the satisfaction of how Memphis got there.

The city's first appearance on ESPN's "College GameDay" was every bit the civic celebration we hoped it would be during the past week of anticipation. It was the rare event that began with considerable expectations and managed to surpass them all.

"It feels like Obama came or something," Memphis Grizzlies star Jaren Jackson Jr. remarked during a brief interview on the show.

"It's one of the great scenes that we've had in a long time," ESPN's Kirk Herbstreit said on social media after the show.

"All I can say is my 58-year-old sister was here at 3:30 in the morning," former Memphis basketball player Kenneth Moody said.

So many arrived on Beale Street when it was still dark out, and some never even left. Alfred's never actually closed its bar.

By the time the "College GameDay" pit opened at 5:30 a.m., the line to get in stretched almost all the way up the block. The first "T-I-G-E-R-S Tigers" chant occurred before 6 a.m. As the show started at 8 o'clock, almost every inch of Beale Street was filled between B.B. King Boulevard and South Second Street. Throughout the show, fans booed any time the University of Tennessee was mentioned.

And almost everyone had a sign.

There were too many to count dedicated to Memphis tight end Joey Magnifico, and the controversial catch reversal that cost Memphis a chance to beat Temple last month.

OPPOSITE: Fans crowd Beale Street on Saturday, Nov. 2, 2019, as ESPN's "College GameDay" came to Memphis for the first time ever.
MAX GERSH / THE COMMERCIAL APPEAL

"We want Bama," one Memphis poster read, "in women's soccer."

"Thank you Jacob Rainey. Sincerely, the city of Memphis," read another, in reference to the Tulsa kicker who missed field goals against the Tigers and SMU in recent weeks, paving the way for this grand stage to come to town.

"Paying players before it was cool (and legal)," read one SMU fan's sign.

And then there was Mike and Donna Malone of Collierville, two Washington State graduates who were waving a giant Washington State flag. Ol' Crimson was overnighted in the mail this week by a Washington State alumni group to ensure it appeared on "College GameDay" for a record 235th show in a row.

The best part? Mike Malone pulled up his coat to reveal a Memphis Tigers T-shirt underneath.

A spotlight on Memphis

At its core, this "College GameDay" was about Memphis, even though it still served as a national pregame show for all of college football.

It showed Graceland and played Elvis Presley's music in and out of commercial breaks. It mentioned the history of Liberty Bowl Memorial Stadium. It made us laugh about Norvell's ill-fated cornrows from Central Arkansas football media day and it made us cry telling the story of Memphis running back Kenneth Gainwell and his older brother who survived a stroke.

It spotlighted St. Jude Children's Research Hospital with a brief shot of Javon Bass, a freshman trombonist in the Memphis marching band who's completed three treatments for leukemia at St. Jude. It showcased Memphis barbecue, and the Memphis Grizzlies, the Memphis Tigers basketball team, and, more significantly,

LEFT: The earliest fans arriving on Beale Street earn orange Home Depot hats and front-row spots for "College GameDay." MAX GERSH / THE COMMERCIAL APPEAL

the Memphis football team.

It also ended with something of an homage to this city's pro wrestling legacy, and Elvis, of course.

There was Corso in a white jumpsuit, a black wig and sunglasses befitting the King of Rock and Roll. Everyone else had picked Memphis to beat SMU. He had just been handed a white flag by Lawler, a nod to the white flag he waved as Louisville's coach when he lost to Memphis, 69-19, at the Liberty Bowl 50 years ago.

Corso praised Memphis and put down SMU all show long, setting up this moment.

"Poor ol' SMU," he said at one point. "Ain't got a chance."

So it made sense when he shouted, "Hand me that Tiger head" to make his pick.

But Corso then held it just over his head for a few seconds before flinging it to the stage floor. On went the SMU Mustang head, and a city that loves its wrestling almost as much as its barbecue and basketball had a new heel to hate.

Which really only made this jubilant day even more fun, and even more memorable for everyone there.

Like Dave Wieland, a 2015 University of Memphis graduate who's now an Army intelligence officer stationed at Fort Campbell. He received a short-notice deployment over the past three weeks, so he drove more than three hours to be on the corner of Beale and B.B. King.

Attending "College GameDay" was one of the last things he'll do before leaving the country for active duty.

"It's no small miracle that this is happening this weekend." Wieland said. "I've waited my whole life for this."

It was a sentiment felt all over Beale Street Saturday morning.

ABOVE: Elvis references adorn many signs across Beale Street. MAX GERSH / THE COMMERCIAL APPEAL

RIGHT: The University of Memphis Mighty Sound of the South performs as ESPN's "College GameDay" airs from Beale Street. MAX GERSH / THE COMMERCIAL APPEAL

Best moments from "College GameDay"

BY EVAN BARNES • THE COMMERCIAL APPEAL

MEMPHIS - Minutes before ESPN's "College GameDay" kicked off, analyst Lee Corso took the stage and played to the enthusiastic Beale Street crowd.

He held helmets from Memphis and SMU, with fans alternating cheers and boos as Corso raised them one at a time. When he dropped SMU's helmet to kiss the Tigers' gray one, the crowd roared.

It was the final spark before the three-hour show began and Memphis reveled in a moment that few thought was possible. The nation's premiere college football show aired live from the city's most well-known street.

Here are the best moments from "College GameDay":

The crowd and signs matched the hype

Beale Street has seen its share of big crowds, but with fans arriving well before 5 a.m., it was one of the biggest for a non-holiday in recent years.

From Second Street to Fourth Street, fans packed the area with signs ranging from the funny ("If Corso was from Memphis, not so fast mane!"), to the ambitious ("Show Me the Cotton Bowl" with Jerry Maguire) to the sarcastic (one thanking Tulsa kicker Jacob Rainey for his missed kick that allowed Memphis to win last week and make "GameDay" happen).

It was made-for-TV spectacle that showed off the best of Memphis prior to the Tigers facing SMU Saturday night

Mike Norvell and his infamous cornrow picture

The Memphis football coach entertained the fans with the show's selfie stick before his appearance on "College GameDay." The crowd got even louder when ESPN brought up a picture of him wearing cornrows during his playing career at Central Arkansas.

Norvell shared how he made a promise to a youth football team he was coaching. If they won, he'd let them braid his hair. They did and thus created one of Norvell's indelible images that endeared him to Tigers fans as much as his success the past four seasons.

Penny Hardaway arrives with Tigers basketball team

It wouldn't be a Memphis party without Penny Hardaway. The Tigers' men's basketball coach showed up in the second hour as his team watched on the balcony of Alfred's.

The crowd cheered "Penny! Penny!" and with the Tigers starting their season on Tuesday, it was a reminder that Memphis athletics as a whole is strong with ranked football, men's basketball

and women's soccer teams.

Jerry Lawler arrives in style

There was no way Jerry "The King" Lawler could arrive without a regal entrance. Lawler, the show's celebrity guest picker, did just that when he arrived in a Batmobile on B.B. King Boulevard

Several fans responded with cheers of "Jerry! Jerry!" as he walked up to the set, although they booed when he picked Tennessee to beat UAB. Naturally, he won them back over by picking Memphis to beat SMU.

Lee Corso fools Memphis fans by picking SMU

Corso's tease before the show felt like foreshadowing and he took it further dressing as Elvis Presley for the picks segment.

After Lawler and Desmond Howard picked Memphis to beat SMU, Corso grabbed the head of Memphis mascot Pouncer and held it high just like he did three hours earlier with the Tigers helmet.

But then, he chucked the head over the "GameDay" desk before putting on SMU's Mustang mascot. The crowd went from loud cheers to jeers and boos at Corso's heel turn, with Lawler reacting with a fake chokehold.

OPPOSITE: Beale Street is the center of college football as "College GameDay" broadcasts live from the Bluff City.
MAX GERSH / THE COMMERCIAL APPEAL

RIGHT: ESPN "College GameDay" host Desmond Howard.
MAX GERSH / THE COMMERCIAL APPEAL

OPPOSITE: Beale Street rocks in the background of ESPN's "College GameDay" as the show came to Memphis for the first time. MAX GERSH / THE COMMERCIAL APPEAL

BELOW RIGHT: Jerry "The King" Lawler joins Lee Corso (dressed as Elvis Presley) as the guest picker for ESPN's "College GameDay." MAX GERSH / THE COMMERCIAL APPEAL

Sports

Coverage Online

For coverage of Memphis' game against SMU, visit commercialappeal.com

5 best moments from 'College GameDay' in Memphis

Evan Barnes
Memphis Commercial Appeal
USA TODAY NETWORK – TENNESSEE

Minutes before ESPN's 'College GameDay' kicked off Saturday morning, analyst Lee Corso took the stage and played to the enthusiastic Beale Street crowd.

He held helmets from Memphis and SMU, with fans alternating cheers and boos as Corso raised them one at a time. When he dropped SMU's helmet to kiss the Tigers' gray one, the crowd roared.

It was the final spark before the three-hour show began and Memphis reveled in a moment that few thought was possible. The nation's premiere college football show aired live from the city's most well-known street.

Here's five of the best moments from 'College GameDay':

The crowd and signs matched the hype

Beale Street has seen its share of big crowds, but with fans arriving well before 5 a.m., it was one of the biggest for a non-holiday in recent years.

From Second Street to Fourth Street, fans packed the area with signs ranging from the funny ("If (Lee) Corso was from Memphis, not so fast man!"), to the ambitious ("Show Me the Cotton Bowl") with Jerry Maguire) to the sarcastic with one thanking Tulsa kicker Jacob Rainey for his missed kick that allowed Memphis to win last week and make

See MOMENTS, Page 6B

Jerry Lawler, left, reacts as Lee Corso puts the Southern Methodist University mascot head Saturday during ESPN "College GameDay" on Beale Street in Memphis. MAX GERSH / THE COMMERCIAL APPEAL

The crowd holds up signs as "College GameDay" is filmed Saturday on Beale Street in downtown Memphis. MAX GERSH / THE COMMERCIAL APPEAL

Living up to expectations

Memphis' 'College GameDay' exceeded the hype

Mark Giannotto
Columnist
Memphis Commercial Appeal
USA TODAY NETWORK – TENN.

Amanda McMinn was standing there with her poster board before Beale Street was completely and astoundingly full of people and signs and flags and just pure, unadulterated fun unlike anything Memphis has ever seen.

This was before Mike Norvell and Penny Hardaway appeared. Before Jerry "The King" Lawler showed up in a Batmobile and Lee Corso dressed up as Elvis for a perfectly executed heel turn. Before the sun had even come up.

"It's wedding anniversary and my husband brought me to College Game-

Day, #besthusbandever," McMinn had written on her sign.

Which is not actually the important part, even though McMinn described this particular anniversary as a "dream" for her and her husband, Mark, who owns Dyer's Burgers.

Because then she introduced her father, Freddie Veteto, who drove overnight from Destin, Florida, to be standing there on the corner of Beale and B.B. King Boulevard Saturday morning, with his daughter and his grandson, Brayden.

Three generations of Memphis fans, scrunched along the sidewalk and street with thousands more just like them, marveling at the history they were witnessing.

"This is like dying and going to heaven," Veteto said. "Never thought the Tigers would get here."

'College GameDay' surpasses the hype

Saturday was about joy and satisfaction. The joy of being there for a once-in-a-lifetime moment in a once-of-a-kind setting, and the satisfaction of how Memphis got there.

The city's first appearance on ESPN's 'College GameDay' was every bit the civic celebration we hoped it would be during the past week of anticipation. It was the rare event that began with considerable expectations and managed to surpass them all.

"It feels like Obama came or something," Memphis Grizzlies star Jaren Jackson Jr. remarked during a brief interview on the show.

"It's one of the great scenes that we've had in a long time," ESPN's Kirk

'We knew we needed to seize that moment'

BY JASON MUNZ • THE COMMERCIAL APPEAL

MEMPHIS - The drive started with 5:31 on the clock in the third quarter.

No. 23 Memphis was ahead of 14th-ranked SMU 33-24, but the Mustangs had just pinned the Tigers deep in their own territory. Their own 2-yard line, to be precise. Kenneth Gainwell, who became the centerpiece of Mike Norvell's prolific offense this season, gained 2 yards on first down. On second down, quarterback Brady White's pass, intended for Damonte Coxie, fell incomplete.

Now, standing in the shadow of their own end zone, in a situation where enough momentum to fill Liberty Bowl Memorial Stadium was potentially hanging in the balance like one of Adam Williams' booming punts, the Tigers needed to make a play. And they needed White to make it.

Spoiler alert.

"We knew we needed to seize that moment," Norvell said after his team's 54-48 win Saturday. "We needed to try to take the momentum. That third-and-8 throw might be one of the best that I've seen Brady make."

The 10-yard dart from White to Gibson was one of four completions for the redshirt junior on that nine-play, 98-yard drive that he capped off with a 24-yard dime over Coxie's inside shoulder for a touchdown that put Memphis up by 16 points. It was a drive that gave the Tigers their biggest lead of the game. Even though the Mustangs eventually narrowed the gap, it was that drive which took a healthy amount of wind out of the visitors' sails.

"Anytime you're pinned up with your back in your own end zone, it takes players to make plays," Norvell said. "We tried to put them in the best position we could, and those guys went out and executed. I thought that was just a huge point in the game."

Facing the third-and-8 situation at their own 4-yard line, White connected with Gibson (who, oh, by the way, finished the game with a school-record 386 all-purpose yards) for 10 yards to move the sticks.

"That play, I saw the coverage. I knew it was, (I) knew what they had coming," White said. "It was part of our third-down plan, so we've been preparing for it all week. I just took my mismatch with A.G. I knew we had good leverage on it. I saw (No.) 2 kind of come down a little bit, because we had our running back swinging and I just threw it out there, gave him a chance.

"It was a big play."

Gibson admits he wasn't sure White's pass had enough touch to avoid being intercepted.

"I was like, 'Is he going to pick it?'" Gibson said. "He got it perfectly over his head and I caught the ball."

OPPOSITE: Memphis Tigers wide receiver Antonio Gibson carries the ball as Southern Methodist University Mustangs linebacker Delano Robinson defends on Nov. 2, 2019, at Liberty Bowl Memorial Stadium. JUSTIN FORD / USA TODAY SPORTS

The same duo hooked up again on the next play, this time for a 16-yard gain out to Memphis' 30-yard line. SMU was flagged for a late hit that advanced the Tigers another 15 yards. Gainwell got Memphis into Mustang territory with an 8-yard run on second down.

But a sack put the Tigers in a fourth-and-3 situation at the SMU 48. No matter, as Norvell went for it and White's 24-yard pass to Calvin Austin III set up the 24-yard touchdown toss to Coxie on the next play.

"Obviously, our O-line and everyone else did a really good job doing their jobs and then finishing out the drive with a touchdown," White said.

RIGHT: Memphis wide receiver Antonio Gibson catches a touchdown pass over against SMU's Chace Cromartie.
JOE RONDONE / THE COMMERCIAL APPEAL

ABOVE: Memphis Tigers quarterback Brady White hands the ball off to Memphis Tigers running back Kenneth Gainwell. JUSTIN FORD / USA TODAY SPORTS

LEFT: Memphis wide receiver Antonio Gibson breaks away from SMU safety Rodney Clemons. JOE RONDONE / THE COMMERCIAL APPEAL

ABOVE: Memphis wide receiver Damonte Coxie looks over at SMU defender Brandon Stephens after catching a pass. JOE RONDONE / THE COMMERCIAL APPEAL

ABOVE RIGHT: Memphis Tigers running back Kenneth Gainwell carries the ball against SMU. JUSTIN FORD / USA TODAY SPORTS

RIGHT: Memphis wide receiver Antonio Gibson dives for the end zone coming up just short at the 1-yard line. JOE RONDONE / THE COMMERCIAL APPEAL

LEFT: Memphis Tigers quarterback Brady White lines up for a play. JUSTIN FORD / USA TODAY SPORTS

BELOW LEFT: Memphis quarterback Brady White throws the ball. JOE RONDONE / THE COMMERCIAL APPEAL

BELOW: Memphis running back Kenneth Gainwell dives forward for extra yards. JOE RONDONE / THE COMMERCIAL APPEAL

ABOVE: Fans celebrate the University of Memphis football team as players take their Tiger Walk to Liberty Bowl Memorial Stadium before playing SMU. JOE RONDONE / THE COMMERCIAL APPEAL

OPPOSITE: Fans fill the Liberty Bowl Memorial Stadium. JOE RONDONE / THE COMMERCIAL APPEAL

RIGHT: Memphis fans show their love for Tigers running back Kenneth Gainwell. JOE RONDONE / THE COMMERCIAL APPEAL

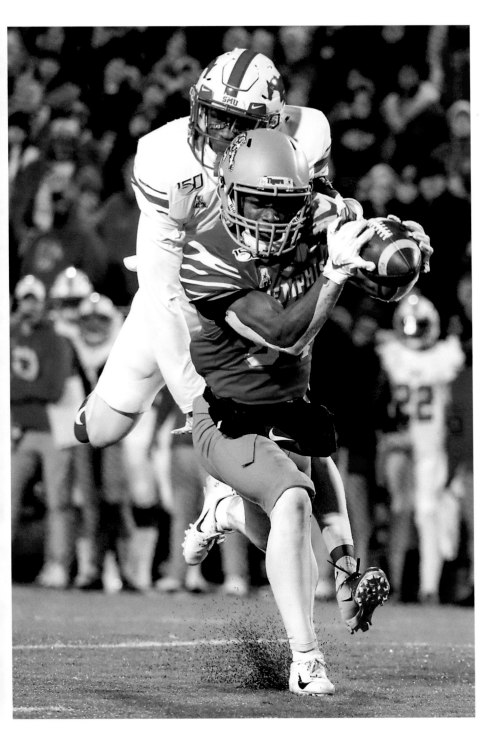

ABOVE: Memphis Xavier "Zay" Cullens and Jonathan Wilson combine to bring down SMU running back Ke'Mon Freeman. JOE RONDONE / THE COMMERCIAL APPEAL

LEFT: Memphis wide receiver Calvin Austin III catches a pass against SMU's Ar'mani Johnson. JOE RONDONE / THE COMMERCIAL APPEAL

OPPOSITE: Memphis Tigers wide receiver Damonte Coxie attempts to catch a pass in front of SMU defensive back Brandon Stephens. JUSTIN FORD / USA TODAY SPORTS

The best day in Memphis football history

BY MARK GIANNOTTO • THE COMMERCIAL APPEAL

> **"Memphis had an opportunity to be showcased today, and much like this football team, it rose to the occasion."**
>
> MIKE NORVELL

MEMPHIS - Mike Norvell paused for a moment to search for the right word.

"Special," he said. "Special."

And that's when his voice began to crack.

When the emotions of seeing Beale Street full of Memphis fans in the morning and seeing Liberty Bowl Memorial Stadium full of Memphis fans in the evening almost got the best of him.

When he allowed himself to consider the goosebumps he got that moment he stepped out of the car and saw the throng of Memphians at ESPN's "College GameDay." When he understood the entire scene surrounding the Tigers' 54-48 win over SMU meant as much to him, and as much to Memphis football, as the win itself.

"This community means a lot to me, and to see that, man, I've been hopeful for it," Norvell said. "But they showed up, and I'm just really proud."

This is how the best day in Memphis football history ended.

The morning belonged to the city of Memphis and the fans and the Beale Street celebration nobody could have predicted a decade ago. The night belonged to this Memphis football team, and the players who put on another show for another awe-inspiring crowd.

There were 59,506 people in the Liberty Bowl — a new record for an American Athletic Conference game. It was a sight to behold, a sight that would have been unfathomable a decade ago. That, frankly, would have seemed unfathomable only a few weeks ago.

This wasn't a stadium half-filled with fans of the opposing SEC team. This was Memphis fans cheering for Memphis. Nobody could remember when it ever felt like this before.

"It's a big deal when we come running out of the tunnel and see that thing packed," Memphis quarterback Brady White said. "It's like a kid in a candy store. It's an awesome feeling, an awesome experience."

It was, in retrospect, the fuel these Tigers needed during a game in which they refused to let any obstacle slow them down.

Not AAC officials who wiped out three first-half touchdowns — just a few weeks after a controversial replay review that factored into the Tigers' lone loss — and earned a consistent cascade of boos.

Not 16 penalties.

Not an undefeated Top 25 opponent whose record helped create the euphoria downtown that preceded the evening's nationally-televised main event, and whose offense couldn't seem to be stopped by the Memphis defense.

So now, no goal is out of reach.

Not a division title. Not an AAC title. Not that coveted New Year's Six bowl bid. It's all right there in front of Memphis.

Because there was White at the 30-yard-line, his arms raised before the touchdown pass even landed in the arms of Damonte Coxie, part of a crucial 98-yard drive in which he threw a beautiful pass out of his own end zone and a beautiful pass to convert a fourth down.

He was rewriting his own narrative by throwing for 350 yards and three touchdowns, dispelling once and for all the notion that existed as recently as a month ago that he can't throw downfield.

There was wide receiver Antonio Gibson, affirming that he's the program's latest playmaker to emerge from Norvell's dynamic offensive scheme, scoring a receiving touchdown, a kickoff return touchdown and a rushing touchdown en route to a school-record 386 all-purpose yards.

There was Coxie, reaffirming his status as one of the AAC's top wide receivers with two touchdown catches that helped the Tigers top SMU's powerful offense.

There was placekicker Riley Patterson, previously known more for the kicks he's missed than the kicks he's made, hitting four field goals when Memphis' offense kept stalling for reasons that oftentimes

seemed to be the result of decisions many of its fans found questionable.

Nothing outside of SMU blowing out Memphis could have ruined what took place on this day. The "College GameDay" party on Beale Street, the pictures of the Liberty Bowl filled to the brim — those will be part of this program's lore for years to come now.

They are confirmation, here in Memphis and throughout the college football world, of what Tigers football has become over the past six years.

"Memphis had an opportunity to be showcased today," Norvell said, "and much like this football team, it rose to the occasion."

But winning or losing this game mattered. A lot.

It mattered because winning this game means Memphis controls its own destiny with three regular-season games left. It mattered because Memphis is now in position to secure a berth in a New Year's Six bowl if it wins the AAC championship.

But it mattered, most of all, because winning makes it more likely this doesn't become a one-off event. That this is not just a fantastic anomaly courtesy of ESPN.

That perhaps this feels closer to the norm moving forward.

Because this game marked the end of a special day in Memphis football history. But it also seemed like the beginning of the stretch run to a special season.

ABOVE: Memphis quarterback Brady White takes a selfie with fans in the stands after their 54-48 win over SMU. JOE RONDONE / THE COMMERCIAL APPEAL

ABOVE LEFT: Memphis wide receiver Antonio Gibson celebrates his touchdown. JOE RONDONE / THE COMMERCIAL APPEAL

OPPOSITE: Memphis long snapper Preston Brady celebrates securing an onside kick against SMU. JOE RONDONE / THE COMMERCIAL APPEAL

LEFT: Memphis running back Timothy Taylor celebrates the win. JOE RONDONE / THE COMMERCIAL APPEAL

White lights up Houston as Tigers continue to roll

BY EVAN BARNES • THE COMMERCIAL APPEAL

HOUSTON - Late in the fourth quarter, Houston's band paid tribute to rapper/pop star Lizzo by playing her hit "Good As Hell" during a Memphis drive.

It summed up No. 18 Memphis' mood after its 45-27 win at TDECU Stadium. A fourth consecutive 40-point performance. A six-touchdown day from Brady White. The return of senior leader Patrick Taylor.

White felt so good, in fact, he ran for his second touchdown of the season: a 14-yard run with nobody in sight except teammates to greet him.

Here's what we learned from Memphis' (9-1, 5-1) fourth consecutive win:

Brady White had the best road game of his career

White's 341 passing yards, his fifth 300-yard game of the season, was exactly what Memphis needed after being off the previous week. His five touchdown passes, which tied a career high, went to four different receivers, including two touchdown catches from Damonte Coxie.

For the second consecutive game, White led the Tigers on a 98-yard scoring drive, this time to end the first half. He showed off his footwork by keeping plays alive and escaping defenders. Not even an early interception slowed his rhythm.

Welcome back, Patrick Taylor

With 9:25 left in the first quarter, Taylor took the field for the first time since being injured against Ole Miss. It was a welcome sight after he spent the past eight games on the sidelines.

Taylor was in on approximately 21 plays and finished with 14 rushing yards on five carries. Kenneth Gainwell took the heavy lifting with 17 carries for 99 yards, but Taylor's presence is a good sign that Memphis' offense is back to full strength.

Calvin Austin III continues to break out

The sophomore wide receiver has come on strong in the Tigers' last three games and he played his best game to date against Houston (3-7, 1-5)

Austin had five catches for 81 yards, all in the first half. He finished the Tigers' 98-yard scoring drive with a 16-yard touchdown catch in the corner of the end zone. After the game, the Memphis native was awarded a scholarship.

Defense returns to form

It looked like the same old Tigers after they gave up a 53-yard touchdown catch and a 68-yard touchdown run by Clayton Tune to start the game. Yet the Tigers buckled down and kept the Cougars in check despite not having senior linebacker Austin Hall, who was out due to injury.

The biggest stop came with the Tigers holding Houston to a field goal after a

---

OPPOSITE: Memphis wide receiver Damonte Coxie, right, celebrates his touchdown with wide receiver Tahj Washington against the University of Houston on Nov. 16, 2019, in Houston. ERIC CHRISTIAN SMITH / AP

9-minute, 22-second drive. On Memphis' next drive, White had his go-ahead touchdown run.

Houston only had 49 yards at halftime, a performance reminiscent of what the Tigers looked like in the first half of the season.

This season continues to be special for Memphis

This Tigers team isn't as explosive as Mike Norvell's 2017 unit but it's quietly etching a place among the best teams in school history.

This victory marked the fourth time in six seasons the Tigers have won at least nine games. It's the fourth consecutive game Memphis has scored at least 40 points. And it put the Tigers in first place in the AAC West with tiebreaker edges over SMU and Navy.

RIGHT: Houston quarterback Clayton Tune, right, is tackled by Memphis linebacker Xavier Cullens.
ERIC CHRISTIAN SMITH / AP

ABOVE: Memphis wide receiver Damonte Coxie scores a touchdown as Houston safety Garrison Vaughn defends. ERIC CHRISTIAN SMITH / AP

ABOVE LEFT: Memphis wide receiver Damonte Coxie makes a catch as Houston cornerback Damarion Williams defends. ERIC CHRISTIAN SMITH / AP

LEFT: Memphis wide receiver Damonte Coxie, right, celebrates his touchdown with quarterback Brady White. ERIC CHRISTIAN SMITH / AP

ABOVE: Houston quarterback Clayton Tune fumbles while being sacked by Memphis linebacker Thomas Pickens.
ERIC CHRISTIAN SMITH / AP

LEFT: Memphis wide receiver Antonio Gibson, right, celebrates his touchdown with offensive lineman Manuel Orona-Lopez as tight end Joey Magnifico watches.
ERIC CHRISTIAN SMITH / AP

OPPOSITE: Memphis wide receiver Antonio Gibson celebrates his touchdown with tight end Joey Magnifico.
ERIC CHRISTIAN SMITH / AP

Setting the table for a showdown

BY EVAN BARNES • THE COMMERCIAL APPEAL

TAMPA, Fla. - Midway through the third quarter at Raymond James Stadium, Memphis and South Florida were interrupted by a gray cat on the field.

The cat raced upfield to the sound of cheering fans before disappearing under a cart.

Just like the cat, No. 18 Memphis had no trouble moving down the field, winning 49-10 in a commanding performance where its offensive starters were pulled near the end of the third quarter.

For the fourth time in program history, the Tigers (10-1, 6-1 AAC) cracked the 10-win mark. They have a chance to clinch their third consecutive AAC West title against Cincinnati (10-1, 7-0).

Here's what we learned from the Tigers' fifth consecutive win:

Memphis' offense is locked in

Not even two early interceptions thrown by Brady White could slow down the Tigers. After White's second interception, he led Memphis on three consecutive scoring drives to end the first half.

White (18-of-28, 222 yards, two touchdowns) showed poise when the Tigers faced a second-and-38 in the second quarter. In two plays, Memphis scored thanks to a 20-yard catch by Damonte Coxie and a 50-yard touchdown grab by Kedarian Jones.

Memphis scored more than 40 points for the fifth consecutive game.

A dangerous duo

If last week was a tease with running back Patrick Taylor's return from injury, this week was a return of Memphis' reliable two-back system with Kenneth Gainwell and Taylor splitting the load.

Taylor, who missed eight games with a foot injury, looked like himself again with three touchdowns and 95 rushing yards on a 17 carries. He also had a 20-yard catch. Gainwell had 128 yards on 14 carries, the first time in three weeks he crossed the 100-yard mark.

Gainwell improved to 1,294 rushing yards this season, the fifth-best single season in Memphis history. But with Taylor finding his form, the Tigers' offense is even more dangerous.

Receiving corps shows balance

For the past three games, a Tigers receiver not named Damonte Coxie has made his presence known: Antonio Gibson, Calvin Austin and now Kedarian Jones.

The senior had a team-high six catches for 99 yards, including the 50-yard touchdown where he spun away from a defender and ran to the end zone. He's had big catches all season and added another stamp on his breakout year.

OPPOSITE: Memphis Tigers wide receiver Antonio Gibson rushes the ball as South Florida Bulls defensive back Devin Studstill readies for contact on Nov. 23, 2019, at Raymond James Stadium in Tampa. REINHOLD MATAY / USA TODAY SPORTS

Tigers' defense impresses again

South Florida (4-7, 2-5) began with a 75-yard scoring drive but ended with just 170 yards of offense.

Linebacker Austin Hall returned after missing a week because of injury, and for the second consecutive week, the Tigers' front seven exerted its will.

Getting ready for a Black Friday showdown

Now that Memphis has won 10 games for the second time under coach Mike Norvell, the Tigers can make some history hosting Cincinnati to close out the regular season. The USF victory put Memphis in position to set a school record for wins in a single season and earn its first AAC championship with a victory over Cincinnati.

RIGHT: Memphis Tigers wide receiver Traveon Samuel runs the ball against USF.
REINHOLD MATAY / USA TODAY SPORTS

LEFT: Tigers running back Patrick Taylor Jr. dives in for the score as USF linebacker Demaurez Bellamy tries to stop him. REINHOLD MATAY / USA TODAY SPORTS

BELOW LEFT: Tigers quarterback Connor Adair runs it in for a 22 yard touchdown as USF linebacker Andrew Mims and linebacker Dwayne Boyles give. REINHOLD MATAY / USA TODAY SPORTS

BELOW: Tigers wide receiver Calvin Austin III runs the ball as USF quarterback Blake Barnett dives for the tackle. REINHOLD MATAY / USA TODAY SPORTS

ABOVE: Memphis Tigers defensive lineman Joseph Dorceus, left, and linebacker JJ Russell, right, combine to stop USF quarterback Jordan McCloud. REINHOLD MATAY / USA TODAY SPORTS

ABOVE RIGHT: South Florida Bulls defensive end Tyrik Jones chases Memphis Tigers quarterback Markevion Quinn. REINHOLD MATAY / USA TODAY SPORTS

RIGHT: A cat held up play as it ran onto the field during the second half. REINHOLD MATAY / USA TODAY SPORTS

Memphis Tigers tight end Kameron Wilson, offensive lineman Michael Denson and wide receiver Tahj Washington celebrate a 22-yard touchdown run by quarterback Connor Adair. REINHOLD MATAY / USA TODAY SPORTS

Tricky play, straightforward result

BY EVAN BARNES • THE COMMERCIAL APPEAL

MEMPHIS - It was a risky call. One that a coach only makes when he trusts his team in a close game.

Facing second-and-7, Memphis football coach Mike Norvell dug deep in his bag of tricks and called a reverse flea flicker. Brady White handed it off to Patrick Taylor, who flipped it to Kedarian Jones. Jones tossed it back to White, who threw a 46-yard touchdown pass to Damonte Coxie.

On a night when Memphis' offense struggled, it was a perfect trick to push the Tigers to a 34-24 win over Cincinnati at Liberty Bowl Memorial Stadium to close out the regular season.

No. 18 Memphis (11-1, 7-1 AAC) swarmed the field to celebrate its third consecutive AAC West championship and set a single-season record for wins. Here's what we learned:

Tigers' offense comes alive

Besides White's trick-play touchdown pass to Coxie, Antonio Gibson sealed the deal with a 29-yard touchdown run with 3:16 left. Coxie finished with a game-high 145 receiving yards on six catches.

Despite an offense that looked anemic in the red zone after settling for two field goals in the first half, Memphis scored twice in the fourth quarter to finish off the Bearcats after a scoreless third quarter.

Second-half defense shows up big

Memphis' defense looked awful on stopping No. 17 Cincinnati (10-2, 7-1) on third downs. But after halftime, the Tigers found renewed life.

The Tigers opened the third quarter by forcing a three-and-out, an interception by Jacobi Francis, a forced fumble by Jonathan Wilson and a turnover on downs. In the fourth quarter, Memphis forced a three-and-out after a late Brady White interception.

Seniors step up on Senior Day

Start with Bryce Huff, who had a stellar day with 3.5 tackles for loss and two forced fumbles. Add in Kedarian Jones' 9-yard touchdown catch in the first quarter.

Finish it off with Gibson's 29-yard touchdown run and the Memphis seniors led a historic night for the Tigers, who won their 500th game in program history.

But wait, there's more

If folks loved Round I between Memphis and Cincinnati, Round II would be even bigger next week

Memphis earned the right to host this same Cincinnati team in the AAC title game. With more wins than in any Tigers season in history, Memphis would be playing for the school's first outright conference championship since 1969 and a chance to play in a New Year's Six bowl.

OPPOSITE: Memphis players hoist the AAC West championship trophy after defeating Cincinnati 34-24 on Nov. 29, 2019, at Liberty Bowl Memorial Stadium in Memphis. MAX GERSH / THE COMMERCIAL APPEAL

ABOVE: Memphis Tigers defensive lineman Morris Joseph Jr. tackles Cincinnati Bearcats running back Michael Warren II. NELSON CHENAULT / USA TODAY SPORTS

ABOVE RIGHT: Memphis Tigers wide receiver Damonte Coxie beats Cincinnati Bearcats cornerback Cam Jefferies for a touchdown catch. NELSON CHENAULT / USA TODAY SPORTS

OPPOSITE: Memphis Tigers wide receiver Kenneth Gainwell runs after a catch as Cincinnati Bearcats defensive back Michael Pitts attempts a tackle. NELSON CHENAULT / USA TODAY SPORTS

RIGHT: Memphis Tigers quarterback Brady White rushes as Cincinnati Bearcats linebacker Perry Young defends. NELSON CHENAULT / USA TODAY SPORTS

ABOVE: Memphis' Damonte Coxie brings in a pass. MAX GERSH / THE COMMERCIAL APPEAL

ABOVE LEFT: Cincinnati Bearcats quarterback Ben Bryant is sacked by Memphis Tigers defensive lineman Joseph Dorceus. NELSON CHENAULT / USA TODAY SPORTS

OPPOSITE: Memphis quarterback Brady White draws back to pass. MAX GERSH / THE COMMERCIAL APPEAL

LEFT: Memphis' Chris Claybrooks runs back the opening kickoff for a touchdown. MAX GERSH / THE COMMERCIAL APPEAL

A matter of faith and belief

BY MARK GIANNOTTO • THE COMMERCIAL APPEAL

MEMPHIS - On the biggest play of the most important game to date during this historic Memphis football season, they all had to believe in each other.

Mike Norvell had to believe in himself, right after he went for it on fourth down when he could have padded the lead and failed. He had to believe the players would execute this trick play. Even though this particular trick play had only been installed two weeks before. Even though the Tigers had only practiced it maybe six or seven times.

Quarterback Brady White had to believe that tailback Patrick Taylor Jr. would successfully flip to the ball to wide receiver Kedarian Jones, and that Jones would then toss it back to White.

White had to believe his eyes, because in practice he didn't usually see wide receiver Damonte Coxie streaking past a defender. He had to believe if he just threw the ball up there, Coxie would catch it.

And Coxie had to believe in White. He had to believe White meant what he said earlier in the game, that the ball was eventually coming his way. He had to believe in himself, that as White's pass soared through the air "me or nobody" was coming down with it.

They had to believe that if this didn't work, if Cincinnati got the ball back, their defense would deliver again.

So after this regular-season finale, after White took the feed from Jones,

after White launched the ball into the air, after Coxie grabbed it in the end zone, after the Tigers secured their 34-24 win over Cincinnati and a third straight spot in the American Athletic Conference championship game, it's time to believe what you're watching.

Because we're witnessing history as it happens. Just think of all this team has accomplished, or could accomplish in just a week's time.

The Tigers have won 11 games for the first time in program history. They're one win from the program's first outright conference championship since 1969 and the biggest bowl game this program has ever experienced. They're hosting the AAC championship game for the first time, against this very same Cincinnati.

They're delivering on almost every preseason expectation, and they still want more.

All of that didn't happen because of that one play because Norvell stayed aggressive when other coaches might not have. But it is why we are where we are now.

Never mind the stakes of the situation. Never mind what conventional wisdom would have suggested. Never mind Norvell's questionable decision to go for it on fourth-and-2 when he could have kicked a field goal just a few minutes earlier.

That bowl game, that one last win, won't validate Norvell or this team. That's

already done. This is the most complete team Memphis has fielded during its six-year resurgence.

This team beat Ole Miss by scoring 15 points to begin the season, but then ended up fielding a top-10 offense. And the victory over Cincinnati encapsulated all of that.

It featured Chris Claybrooks taking the opening kickoff back for a touchdown, more than 400 yards of offense and a defense that took control of the second half.

The 36,472 in attendance seemed to recognize that, breaking out a thunderous "Let's go Tigers" chant with less than four minutes to go, right before Antonio Gibson iced this game with one last touchdown run.

"You can't be a great team if you just have a good side of the ball, or a couple of good players," Norvell said.

So the postgame celebration was different than the past two years. It was muted by design, Norvell said, because "we're not done."

"We know that that was a great accomplishment and it was great for the fans and for the program," Coxie said. "But there's another that we want."

They all believe there's more to accomplish.

ABOVE: Memphis Tigers runningback Kenneth Gainwell rushes as quarterback Brady White looks on. NELSON CHENAULT / USA TODAY SPORTS

ABOVE RIGHT: Kenneth Gainwell rushes against Cincinnati. MAX GERSH / THE COMMERCIAL APPEAL

RIGHT: Tigers defensive back Quindell Johnson dives to bring down Cincinnati tight end Josiah Deguara. MAX GERSH / THE COMMERCIAL APPEAL

Memphis Tigers wide receiver Damonte Coxie celebrates after catching a touchdown pass.

LEFT: Memphis Tigers defensive back Chris Claybrooks wraps up Cincinnati's Thomas Geddis. MAX GERSH / THE COMMERCIAL APPEAL

OPPOSITE: Tigers wide receiver Damonte Coxie looks back while running the ball after making a catch. MAX GERSH / THE COMMERCIAL APPEAL

BELOW FAR LEFT: Tigers wide receiver Antonio Gibson looks to move the ball past Cincinnati's Ahmad Gardner. MAX GERSH / THE COMMERCIAL APPEAL

BELOW LEFT: Memphis head coach Mike Norvell pats quarterback Brady White's helmet as he comes back to the sideline after passing for a touchdown. MAX GERSH / THE COMMERCIAL APPEAL

ABOVE: Memphis Tigers players hold the American Athletic Conference West Division Champion trophy after their win over Cincinnati. NELSON CHENAULT / USA TODAY SPORTS

RIGHT: Memphis head coach Mike Norvell hoists the AAC West championship trophy.

MAX GERSH / THE COMMERCIAL APPEAL

Three years in the making

BY EVAN BARNES • THE COMMERCIAL APPEAL

MEMPHIS - Memphis running back Kenneth Gainwell sat on the sideline with a towel on his head, unable to watch Cincinnati's final fourth-down play in the AAC championship game.

Tigers quarterback Brady White walked over to receiver Damonte Coxie to watch the play with him.

Gainwell said a prayer as he thought about how the Memphis Tigers got to this point. White was planning to tell Coxie, who had a game-high 165 receiving yards, he was still a champion.

When Cincinnati quarterback Desmond Ridder's pass sailed high out of bounds, all three joined their teammates in a wild celebration over the 29-24 win. The Tigers reveled in being AAC champions for the second time in school history and first time outright.

"I was all over the place," Gainwell said. "I'm just real proud for this team. From January to now we worked extremely hard to get to where we at right now. We deserved it."

Fake cigars were passed out on the field, and several players left the locker room with them still in their mouths. The official announcement wouldn't come until a day later, but they knew they were headed to the Cotton Bowl.

"Dallas, Texas. Jerry World. We're going to be there," senior Joey Magnifico said.

It was a celebration three years in the making after the Tigers (12-1) came up short the previous two AAC championship games to UCF. As the players walked to greet family and friends, they were relieved to finally have a chance to raise a trophy in December.

All season long, coach Mike Norvell said he was proud of how the team responded when challenged. Although there were reports emerging that he had already accepted the Florida State coaching job, the Memphis players thought about his message as they walked around with AAC championship hats.

"It's hard to keep going back-to-back and coming up short and still try to find that drive to come do it again," Coxie said. "I just salute all my teammates. Them boys keep fighting and fighting and we're just blessed to have this feeling and be champs."

Antonio Gibson, who was named the game's most outstanding player with 234 all-purpose yards, thought of the offseason workouts and how he saw his teammates motivated by losing a 17-point lead to UCF in last year's AAC championship game.

When Norvell leaned on him as the team's most reliable running back, he delivered in a similar fashion that he did against SMU. The senior had his first 100-yard rushing game and caught the go-ahead touchdown.

"I put it in my head that we were going to leave with that trophy," Gibson said. "Going down toward that last drive, I had a feeling in my head that nobody was going to stop me."

"The last two years put a chip on everybody's shoulder. We came up short and we knew we were capable of winning that game. The workouts, the lifting, the

---

OPPOSITE: Memphis Tigers head coach Mike Norvell celebrates the Tigers' 29-24 AAC Championship win over Cincinnati at Liberty Bowl Memorial Stadium on Dec. 7, 2019. JOE RONDONE / THE COMMERCIAL APPEAL

running, everybody had that edge. There was no kind of slacking and it paid off."

During Norvell's four-year tenure, winning became the new standard. But Memphis had yet to add a conference championship or a bowl win to its trophy case.

Now that the Tigers have, there's one last prize they want. The Tigers have not won a bowl game since 2014.

"I'm getting a little spoiled (reaching bowl games) but we got to leave one with a W. I lost every other one so I'm trying to get that W," Magnifico said.

OPPOSITE: Memphis Tigers running back Patrick Taylor Jr. celebrates a first down run against Cincinnati. JOE RONDONE / THE COMMERCIAL APPEAL

Memphis wins AAC

Memphis wide receiver Antonio Gibson (14) breaks away from the pack to run for a touchdown during the AAC Championship game against Cincinnati at Liberty Bowl Memorial Stadium in Memphis, Tenn., on Saturday. HENRY TAYLOR/THE LEAF-CHRONICLE

Tigers grab conference title in likely Norvell's last game

Evan Barnes
Memphis Commercial Appeal
USA TODAY NETWORK – TENNESSEE

Memphis is no stranger to December heartbreak, having lost all five games in the month under Mike Norvell.

On Saturday, the Tigers said goodbye to past ghosts in dramatic fashion. An-tonio Gibson caught a bubble screen touchdown with 1:14 left and Liberty Bowl Memorial Stadium erupted in wild cheers.

A fourth-down penalty by Cincinnati erased the demons for good and Mem-phis celebrated its long-awaited first outright AAC championship with a 29-24 win.

Memphis coach Mike Norvell raised his hands in joy after being doused by Gatorade. Players hugged each other on the field and Chris Claybrooks went to the south end zone and did two running backflips.

Here's what we learned from the Ti-gers (12-1) winning their first outright conference championship since 1969.

Mike Norvell has likely coached his last Memphis game

The Tallahassee Democrat, among others, reported Saturday that Florida State is expected to name Norvell as coach as early as Sunday. It had been

See TIGERS, Page 3B

Kiffin becomes coach at Ole Miss, steps down at FAU

Tim Reynolds
AP SPORTS WRITER

BOCA RATON, Fla. – Lane Kiffin is

sons. It had been college football's worst-kept secret since Friday, and the schools ended all doubt Saturday af-ternoon by announcing the move.

If there was any doubt when Satur-day began, it went away once a short video clip of his son's reaction to the

"Let's go!" Knox Kiffin responds, be-fore chanting "S-E-C! S-E-C!"

Indeed, the SEC is gaining a top

ABOVE: Memphis Tigers wide receiver Antonio Gibson breaks away from Cincinnati linebacker Perry Young. JOE RONDONE / THE COMMERCIAL APPEAL

ABOVE LEFT: Memphis wide receiver Antonio Gibson sprints the sidelines for a touchdown. JOE RONDONE / THE COMMERCIAL APPEAL

OPPOSITE: University of Memphis mascot Pouncer during the Tiger Walk before the AAC Championship game. JOE RONDONE / THE COMMERCIAL APPEAL

LEFT: Memphis Tigers quarterback Brady White scrambles out of the pocket as Cincinnati Bearcats linebacker Perry Young defends. JOE RONDONE / THE COMMERCIAL APPEAL

RIGHT: Kenneth Gainwell runs the ball. JOE RONDONE / THE COMMERCIAL APPEAL

OPPOSITE: Memphis Tigers offensive lineman Dylan Parham blocks against the Cincinnati defensive line. JOE RONDONE / THE COMMERCIAL APPEAL

BELOW RIGHT: Memphis wide receiver Damonte Coxie celebrates after making a catch. HENRY TAYLOR / THE COMMERCIAL APPEAL

BELOW: Memphis Punter Adam Williams applauds a contacting the kicker call by the referees against Cincinnati. JOE RONDONE / THE COMMERCIAL APPEAL

ABOVE: Memphis wide receiver Antonio Gibson breaks away from the pack to run for a touchdown. HENRY TAYLOR / THE COMMERCIAL APPEAL

LEFT: Memphis Tigers quarterback Brady White throws the ball. JOE RONDONE / THE COMMERCIAL APPEAL

OPPOSITE: Memphis Tigers Antonio Gibson celebrates a first down. JOE RONDONE / THE COMMERCIAL APPEAL

So much more than a final score

BY MARK GIANNOTTO • THE COMMERCIAL APPEAL

MEMPHIS - Amidst the postgame chaos and confetti at Liberty Bowl Memorial Stadium, some Memphis football players left the field on their volition and some had to be forced to leave this scene of pure joy.

But inevitably, before each of them reached the garage door leading into the home locker room, they encountered 70-year-old Don Houston. He's been coming to Tiger football games for 52 years, sitting in section 104, row 65, and seat 16.

Which also means he remembers the last time Memphis won an outright conference championship. Never before, though, had Houston left the stands and come onto the turf after a game. Not until Memphis finally won the American Athletic Conference championship game.

"Thank you guys," he said to one group of players. "I've waited a long time. I'm an old man."

Memphis 29, Cincinnati 24. It is so much more than just a final score.

Because Florida State may be able to take the Memphis football coach. But it can never take away this day, or this moment, or this championship from Memphis. It can never take away the Cotton Bowl that comes along with this latest triumph.

So finally, after nearly four hours, after a draining week of speculation and a drama-filled afternoon of football, this historic Tiger football team began a celebration some in this city have hoped for since 1969.

When Cincinnati's last pass fell incomplete, Mike Norvell raised his arms in the air and was mobbed by coaches and players alike. By the time he reached midfield to shake hands with Cincinnati's Luke Fickell, he'd been given two Gatorade baths.

Cornerback Chris Claybrooks did backflips. Quarterback Brady White embraced wide receiver Damonte Coxie and told him he was a champion. Running back Kenny Gainwell went from draping a towel over his head in prayer to running up and down the sideline.

The most accomplished team in Memphis football history got what it deserved. Norvell got what he deserved, even if he'll be introduced as Florida State's new head coach less than 24 hours after he got it.

And, not to be lost in all of this, the Memphis football fans who have been here all along got what they deserved. This is why they sat through all those losses, and why they never lost faith when the Tigers couldn't quite seem to get over the hump the past two years in this championship game.

This is a memory that will outlast any coach or any player.

"That's what makes the city of Memphis incredible. It's what makes this job so incredible," Norvell said. "You represent something that's special. For anybody on the outside who's never lived in Memphis, you just don't understand."

There was no avoiding some level of awkwardness, though.

The initial reports of Norvell's impending departure began emanating out of the Florida panhandle several hours before the most important game in Memphis football history kicked off.

The idea that this would be his final game began days before that.

The news conference was officially announced by Florida State in the middle of the third quarter, and Bobby Bowden had given his seal of approval by the fourth quarter.

The notion that this would ruin what should have been a glorious day began before that, when Memphis struggled through an uneven first half.

But then it didn't. Then, all of the work Norvell did for this program began to shine through.

White, the quarterback Norvell met in 2012, who he brought from Arizona State and backed even in the face of harsh criticism, began to complete passes. Coxie, the wide receiver Norvell took on after LSU discarded him, kept catching passes.

Antonio Gibson, the junior college wide receiver Norvell added last year, made plays as a running back. Gainwell, the running back Norvell signed over Ole Miss, made plays as a receiver.

Riley Patterson, the kicker Norvell believed in after two straight AAC

> ## "You represent something that's special. For anybody on the outside who's never lived in Memphis, you just don't understand."
>
> — MIKE NORVELL

championship games in which he missed crucial field goals, continued to be obscenely accurate on field goals longer than 50 yards. Claybrooks, the cornerback Norvell thrust back into the lineup after missing the first half of this season with an injury, forced another turnover.

Adam Fuller, the defensive coordinator Norvell hired this offseason, decided to bring pressure in the game's key moments and told his players, "You know what? It's time."

"When it didn't look good in that first half, I believed in these guys," Norvell said, "and that's all we talked about at halftime."

So eventually this nail-biter of a game came down to one clutch touchdown drive and one nerve-wracking defensive stand. It came down to Norvell's decision to throw when others would have run the clock down. It came down to Gibson catching a bubble screen for a go-ahead touchdown.

It came down to fourth down and one pass rush and one final Cincinnati incompletion that sent this Liberty Bowl crowd into absolute pandemonium.

"When we got here there was a lot of change, a lot of questions. People didn't know who I was," Norvell said.

Well, they certainly do now.

Now, this party of a season will rage on to Dallas and Jerry World for the Cotton Bowl. What else is to come, or who the next coach might be, could wait.

Everybody knew this was the end. It's why Norvell was so emotional, his voice cracking each time he reflected on this season. But this was also about this team and this city. So, of course, this was about people like Don Houston.

He was standing there outside the locker room still when the AAC championship trophy was carried in by a group of Memphis players.

"I just wish I'd brought my phone," Houston lamented. "I didn't take any pictures."

Don't worry, though. This title, this moment, they will last forever. And nobody can take that away.

ABOVE: Memphis wide receiver Antonio Gibson celebrates after running the final touchdown of the game that would seal victory for Memphis. HENRY TAYLOR / THE COMMERCIAL APPEAL

OPPOSITE: Memphis Tigers head coach Mike Norvell celebrates after the game.
JUSTIN FORD / USA TODAY SPORTS

RIGHT: Memphis Tigers players LaDarius Jordan, from left, Keith Brigham and Markevion Quinn celebrate the second straight win over Cincinnati. JOE RONDONE / THE COMMERCIAL APPEAL

BELOW RIGHT: Memphis Tigers players celebrate the win. JOE RONDONE / THE COMMERCIAL APPEAL

BELOW: Memphis Tigers wide receiver Tahj Washington celebrates the win. JOE RONDONE / THE COMMERCIAL APPEAL

ABOVE: Memphis Tigers head coach Mike Norvell celebrates their win. JOE RONDONE / THE COMMERCIAL APPEAL

ABOVE LEFT: Memphis wide receiver Kedarian Jones embraces a teammate after securing their AAC Championship win. HENRY TAYLOR / THE COMMERCIAL APPEAL

LEFT: Memphis Tigers linebacker Xavier Cullens celebrates the win. JOE RONDONE / THE COMMERCIAL APPEAL

ABOVE RIGHT: Memphis players hold up the AAC Championship trophy after taking the win over Cincinnati. HENRY TAYLOR / THE COMMERCIAL APPEAL

OPPOSITE: Memphis Tigers players celebrate the win. JOE RONDONE / THE COMMERCIAL APPEAL

BELOW RIGHT: Memphis defensive lineman Wardalis Ducksworth watches the coaches interviews and confetti fly in the air after winning the AAC Championship. HENRY TAYLOR / THE COMMERCIAL APPEAL

Norvell has gone, but should be celebrated

BY MARK GIANNOTTO • THE COMMERCIAL APPEAL

MEMPHIS - Mike Norvell is gone and off to Florida State as almost everyone expected he would be as the past week progressed.

But he won't be forgotten any time soon. Or at least he shouldn't be.

And not just because he won more games than any Memphis football coach before him did during any four-year span. Not just because he led the Tigers to their first outright conference championship in 50 years, or got them to the Cotton Bowl, or earned three straight division titles.

All that success is part of his legacy here, of course. But in the grand scheme of this program, of where it goes now that it must find Norvell's replacement, his impact could be felt for years to come.

Because in Norvell, Memphis has a template for what it needs in a football coach.

What should Memphis' next coach be?

The person who potentially fits that mold could be an in-house candidate like interim coach Ryan Silverfield. Or it could be a Norvell disciple like Notre Dame offensive coordinator Chip Long or Georgia defensive coordinator Dan Lanning. Or it could be someone with head coaching experience like Louisiana's Billy Napier or former Missouri coach Barry Odom.

But the mold is set now.

Memphis needs a coach who can put out an entertaining product and pile up points with prolific offenses to help fill a stadium that's too big for its primary tenant, and to stay ahead of a conference known for its offense.

That's what Norvell did. Memphis was one of four schools in the country to rank among the top 10 in total offense the past three years, and each of those offenses featured different stars and different strengths.

Memphis needs a coach who can find hidden gems in recruiting, who can get creative to fill the roster with more talent than its counterparts, and who can then figure out how to effectively showcase all that talent.

That's what Norvell did. Just look at some of the starters in the AAC championship game and throughout this season. Quarterback Brady White started his career at Arizona State. Wide receiver Damonte Coxie was originally slated to go to LSU. Running back Kenny Gainwell picked Memphis over Ole Miss.

Defensive lineman Jonathan Wilson almost went to Tulane. Left tackle Obinna Eze and cornerback T.J. Carter came from Nashville and chose Memphis over SEC offers. Wide receiver Antonio Gibson came from the junior college ranks, and so did defensive lineman Everitt Cunningham. Safety La'Andre Thomas was a quarterback in high school.

Memphis also needs a coach with a dynamic public persona who will embrace this close-knit community and become one of us, for however long they're here.

That's what Norvell did. He understood how this city's identity is tied, in part, to its university's athletics teams, and how much joy this football program can bring to the people here.

Heck, he even called himself a

OPPOSITE: Memphis Tigers head coach Mike Norvell celebrates with his team on their AAC Championship win over Cincinnati.

JOE RONDONE / THE COMMERCIAL APPEAL

Memphian last month, right after Liberty Bowl Memorial Stadium was filled to the brim with blue-clad Tiger football fans for a nationally televised game and "College GameDay" created a Beale Street party unlike any this town had experienced.

"Everything is moving in the right direction," Norvell said after the AAC championship game win over Cincinnati. "It's so important, this program, for the city, because this city needs Tiger athletics to represent it in a certain way."

Norvell did all of that, and it should help put in perspective whatever disappointment you're feeling right now about his departure. It should also prompt the decision makers at Memphis to not limit their options during this coaching search, to not simply assume the only way to continue this momentum is by hiring someone who's been associated with Norvell.

Because Norvell wasn't tied to Justin Fuente. Even though without Fuente, Norvell might not have come. He might not have been as successful as he became. But it was Norvell who elevated this program to heights that will serve this athletic department for years to come.

How will Norvell be remembered?

Just go over to the Memphis football facility on campus, where there are new offices and the beams and roof of the football program's long-awaited indoor practice facility are already up.

If there's no Norvell, if he doesn't make this team and this program as nationally relevant as he did, who knows if that sort of progress occurs? Who knows if we get to witness so many of these historic moments, the sort of memorable experiences that create lifetime fans?

There were the fantastic home wins over UCLA and Navy in 2017, the run to that first AAC championship game and the exhilarating double-overtime showdown with UCF. There were the four straight wins a year ago that got Memphis back to the AAC championship game, when just about everyone else figured the season was lost.

And there was this magical year, a year that featured a program-record for wins, a national audience seemingly week after week, and finally that elusive league title. He accomplished just about everything one can accomplish at Memphis given the restraints of the current college football landscape.

But more than that, almost everything Norvell did seemed to have the right touch.

Like his decision to have the program buy each player a new suit to wear on game day every season so they looked professional during the team's Tiger Walk but also so they had a full wardrobe of suits by the time they graduated.

Or the way he incorporated former Memphis football players the day before every home game, allowing them to walk the field with the current players and speak to the team.

Or the pictures he had every player put up in their locker, to give them a daily reminder of who they play for.

It all fit. It all contributed to a culture that Memphis can't let slip away with this next hire.

Norvell may gone, but he can't be forgotten.

Meet the new coach, Ryan Silverfield

BY EVAN BARNES AND MARK GIANNOTTO • THE COMMERCIAL APPEAL

MEMPHIS - For almost 20 seconds, Ryan Silverfield was silent. Visibly emotional, he searched for the right words that his emotions wouldn't let him say.

His eyes scanned the room as he nodded his head several times. He held back tears that eventually came during his introduction as Memphis' 25th head football coach.

Finally, he spoke with short adjectives. Honored. Humbled. Grateful. Sincere. Appreciative.

After four seasons as the Tigers' offensive line coach and adding titles such as run game coordinator in 2018 and deputy head coach this season, Silverfield couldn't hide how proud he was to begin his first college football head coaching job.

"We will make this city proud. We will make the University of Memphis proud. All of our fans, thank you. We will make you proud," Silverfield said inside the Billy J. Murphy Football Complex. "I'm excited about this journey for many, many years to come. I can't wait to get started even though I feel like I've already gotten started."

Silverfield, whose first game will be coaching the Tigers in the Cotton Bowl, replaces Mike Norvell, who was 38-15 in four seasons. Norvell led the Tigers to their first outright AAC championship this season before being hired to be the head coach at Florida State after the league title game.

Silverfield, 39, was offered the job Thursday night according to athletic director Laird Veatch. Veatch did not reveal who else was interviewed but said that Silverfield impressed him with his plan for the team.

When he spoke to the Memphis football team Sunday, Veatch had players write on notecards the qualities they wanted in a head coach. Somebody that's real. A competitor. A winner. High energy. Somebody that truly loved and cared for them. A Memphian.

The last quality stood out to Veatch and the search committee during their interview with Silverfield.

"I knew going into that meeting that Ryan loved his players and they loved him," Veatch said. "What I came out of that meeting with is a clear understanding that he can also hold them accountable and do it the right way."

The love was evident when Silverfield was introduced in a private team meeting prior to this press conference. Loud cheers and applause were heard from outside as Silverfield said he embraced most of the team individually.

"That's where the joy comes from," Silverfield said. "To see those young men that I will have the opportunity to lead along with the rest of our staff with a sense of genuine excitement for me to be

their next head coach. Pure joy. It warms my heart."

Silverfield's work with the offensive lineman helped bolster a Tigers' running attack that produced four 1,000-yard rushers the past three seasons. In his first year as run game coordinator, the Tigers set school records with 3,919 rushing yards and 48 rushing touchdowns in 2018.

He's also the last remaining member of Norvell's first staff and began a pipeline of recruiting players in Nashville, including current Tigers T.J. Carter, Obinna Eze, Chris Claybrooks, Rodney Owens and Jashon Watkins-Perkins.

Silverfield also spent six seasons with the Minnesota Vikings (2008-13) as an offensive quality control assistant, defensive line assistant and assistant offensive line coach. In 2015, he spent seven games with the Detroit Lions as an assistant offensive line coach.

Prior to his departure, Norvell spoke well of Silverfield's impact on the program.

"Ryan does a wonderful job building relationships. It's really helped elevate this program alongside me," Norvell said after the AAC title game. "He lives the things we talk about and he's a special leader of men."

Silverfield, in turn, thanked Norvell for giving him the opportunity to be in Memphis. Although Silverfield hails

MAX GERSH / THE COMMERCIAL APPEAL

from Florida, he quickly embraced being a Memphian. He spoke of wanting to continue relationships that he had built in his four seasons. And he spoke about the pride of representing the city.

Now, as he stood ready to lead the program into its next chapter, he reflected on his journey. How he went from making $5,000 a year and sleeping on a cot to getting phone calls ignored when he sought other jobs.

As emotional as he was to be the Tigers' next coach, he was resolute in what he expected his tenure to look like.

"I've always said if you keep swinging that ax good things will come," Silverfield said. "And I'll take that same approach here every single day. We're going to swing, we're going to keep swinging, and we're going to have a lot of success in everything we do here because of that."

OPPOSITE: Fans cheer on the Tigers during the Tiger Walk before the AAC Championship game against Cincinnati. JOE RONDONE / THE COMMERCIAL APPEAL

Penn State won the game, but Memphis won our hearts

BY MARK GIANNOTTO • THE COMMERCIAL APPEAL

ARLINGTON, Texas - When it was over, when this wonderfully historic Memphis football season finished with a wonderfully historic Cotton Bowl game that featured everything but the happy ending, the Memphis football team walked over to the sea of blue in the stands.

They pointed to the crowd and the crowd stood one more time, for one more standing ovation. And they kept clapping until every Memphis football player walked through the tunnel the locker room at AT&T Stadium.

Add that to the list of unforgettable memories that will define this journey far more than Penn State 53, Memphis 39.

The win over Ole Miss that started it all. The scene on Beale Street at "College GameDay" in the morning and the sold-out crowd full of Tiger blue against SMU at night. The first win over Cincinnati that brought the AAC championship game to Memphis for the first time. The second win over Cincinnati that brought an AAC title to Memphis for the first time and brought the Tigers here.

To the place known as Jerry World, under the spotlight of a New Year's Six bowl, in front of a Memphis crowd that reflected the significance of this moment. Tiger blue dwarfed Penn State white, with more than 20,000 Memphis fans (it felt and sounded like a lot more) filling almost an entire side and both end zones of this sparkling venue unlike any other in the country.

"We did this," quarterback Brady White told his teammates as they took the field and took in this remarkable scene during warm-ups.

Suddenly, the chaos of the past month, the coaches who left and the coaches who were calling plays for the first time this season, all of it faded to the background.

Suddenly, we were all reminded, if we ever forgot, to savor the fact that no Memphis football team has ever done what this team did. That games and days like this one aren't guaranteed in the future.

"It was awesome to run out, get to that stadium and see a bunch of blue," White said after the game.

And boy did Memphis deliver for all of them, with twists and turns that were glorious and gut-wrenching and ultimately burnished — and didn't tarnish — the Tigers' reputation.

There was the intriguing first quarter, when Memphis gained more yards than anyone had against Penn State in a first quarter this year and led 13-7. When it spread out Penn State's ferocious front seven with five-receiver formations and quick throws. When White answered Penn State running back Journey Brown's

OPPOSITE: Memphis Tigers take the field for the Goodyear Cotton Bowl Classic against Penn State University at AT&T Stadium in Arlington, Texas, on Dec. 28, 2019. MAX GERSH / THE COMMERCIAL APPEAL

foreboding 32-yard touchdown featuring a highlight-reel stiff-arm with perhaps the finest throw of his career.

An awful second quarter followed, when Memphis shanked punts, committed penalties and gained minus-18 yards on its first three drives. When Penn State began to mash the Tigers' defense on the ground and its last four drives of the first half were all touchdowns.

When Memphis emerged from that with another beautiful throw from White to Damonte Coxie, and another field goal by Riley Patterson, who was still limping after the game due to an ankle injury he suffered earlier this week in practice.

"Response is what defines you," former Memphis coach Mike Norvell tweeted in the midst of all of this.

He was watching, just like every Tiger fan was watching, just like the players and fans at the Memphis basketball game back at FedExForum were watching, when those words rang true again.

Just like they have all season long.

"I don't want anybody getting on our plane with their eyes down, not being proud of what they are," new coach Ryan Silverfield said after the game.

"This was a team that we knew was going to come into this game confident and expecting to win," added Penn State coach James Franklin, "... and they played like that."

This all surfaced again when an inspiring third quarter arrived, when White caught a pass from wide receiver Kedarian Jones to set up one touchdown. When Patterson nailed even more field goals to set Cotton Bowl and NCAA records, and Memphis scored more points than anyone had this season against Penn State's defense.

When the Memphis defense finally came through, when the momentum finally shifted back toward the Tigers after defensive lineman Morris Joseph and Sanchez Blake stood up Brown on

fourth-and-1. When it switched right back just a few plays later.

When Penn State All-America linebacker Micah Parsons applied pressure on White yet again, White attempted an ill-advised shovel pass and Penn State safety Garrett Taylor returned it for a touchdown.

That play proved insurmountable. Penn State churned out third-down conversions, Memphis kicked too many field goals instead of scoring touchdowns and White threw another interception to halt the Tigers' last gasp.

Memphis' 479 passing yards had been offset by Penn State's 396 rushing yards.

"I'm just so frustrated because I feel like we really could've won that game," White said. "I'm probably one of the most frustrated guys right now, but at the same time I recognize the opportunity that we just took advantage of and the performance we put out, which isn't to our standards. But there was a lot to be proud of. It was a slugfest."

It was a fight, at least on this day, that ultimately went to the Big Ten powerhouse with the five-star recruits. Penn State was just a little bit better than the program that rose from the depths of college football to become a Group of Five darling.

But the better story? The more memorable journey?

That belongs to Memphis. Today, tomorrow and forever. Whether Silverfield gets Memphis back to this point or not.

So of course, when this historic season full of new milestones and new narratives ended, the tens of thousands of Tiger fans who flocked to Texas rose one last time.

Maybe Memphis didn't deserve the game. But it deserved the salute.

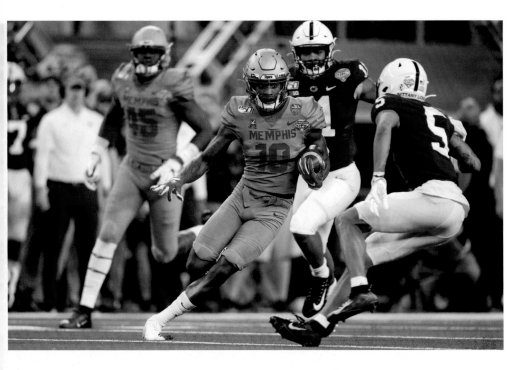

LEFT: Memphis Tigers wide receiver Damonte Coxie runs after a catch against the Penn State Nittany Lions. TIM HEITMAN / USA TODAY SPORTS

OPPOSITE: Memphis quarterback Brady White rushes the ball. MAX GERSH / THE COMMERCIAL APPEAL

BELOW LEFT: Memphis Tigers running back Patrick Taylor Jr. celebrates with tight end Tyce Daniel after scoring a touchdown. KEVIN JAIRAJ / USA TODAY SPORTS

BELOW: Tigers wide receiver Kedarian Jones rushes down the sideline as Penn State's Marquis Wilson (8) and Micah Parsons (11) chase. MAX GERSH / THE COMMERCIAL APPEAL

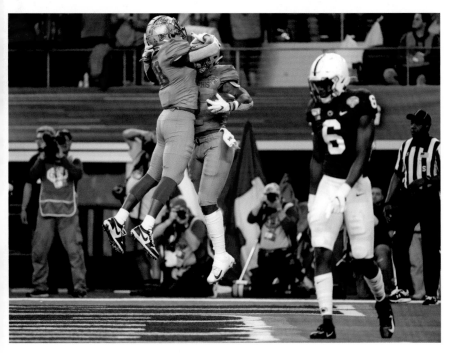

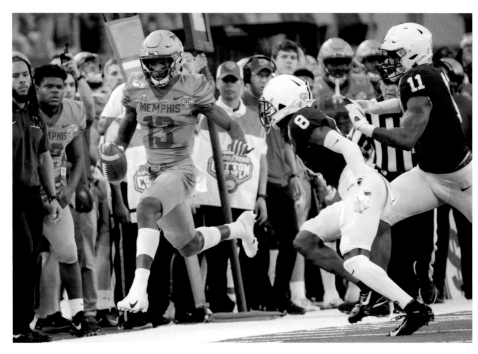

LEFT: Tigers running back Patrick Taylor Jr. dives into the end zone for a touchdown. MAX GERSH / THE COMMERCIAL APPEAL

OPPOSITE RIGHT: Memphis Tigers long snapper Preston Brady reacts after a field goal. KEVIN JAIRAJ / USA TODAY SPORTS

OPPOSITE TOP LEFT: Patrick Taylor Jr. rushes the ball. MAX GERSH / THE COMMERCIAL APPEAL

OPPOSITE BOTTOM LEFT: Memphis defensive end Everitt Cunningham tackles Penn State's Journey Brown in the end zone for a touchdown. MAX GERSH / THE COMMERCIAL APPEAL

BELOW FAR LEFT: Memphis Tigers running back Kenneth Gainwell reacts to a first down. TIM HEITMAN / USA TODAY SPORTS

BELOW LEFT: Kenneth Gainwell stiff arms Penn State's Cam Brown. MAX GERSH / THE COMMERCIAL APPEAL

This time, the Tigers couldn't overcome

BY EVAN BARNES • THE COMMERCIAL APPEAL

ARLINGTON, Texas - Three times this season before facing Penn State at the Cotton Bowl, Memphis had trailed at halftime. Three times, the Tigers rallied for wins.

Memphis tried to make it four against the Nittany Lions. After a season of remarkable highs, another rally would have been fitting for a team that showed its mettle in close games.

Penn State snuffed that hope out in the fourth quarter with a five-minute scoring drive. Memphis lost, 53-39, in Ryan Silverfield's debut as head coach as the Tigers (12-2) lost for the first time since October.

Here's what we learned at AT&T Stadium:

Micah Parsons proved why he's an All-American

The sophomore linebacker's biggest play was forcing Brady White into an interception returned for a touchdown in the third quarter, extending Penn State's lead to 45-36.

He shined all game, from blowing up a Calvin Austin reverse to forcing two fumbles in the first half. Although Memphis scored the most points Penn State allowed all season, Parsons finished with 14 tackles, including two sacks, and two pass breakups.

Fittingly, he was named the Cotton Bowl's most outstanding defensive player.

Memphis couldn't stop the run

It was a bad omen when Penn State's (11-2) first run was Journey Brown breaking four tackles for a 32-yard touchdown. It got worse in the second quarter when Memphis blitzed its safeties and Brown scored on a 56-yard run.

Penn State rushed for 396 yards, with Brown finishing with 202. Noah Cain finished with 90 yards and hit Memphis with a final dagger on a 1-yard touchdown run with 6:31 left.

Brady White had a mixed day in perhaps his final game

White had career highs in attempts (50) and passing yards (454) but had two interceptions. He didn't throw a touchdown pass but ran for a score after setting it up by catching a 25-yard pass from Kedarian Jones.

He became the second quarterback in Memphis history to pass for more than 4,000 yards in a season, joining Riley Ferguson.

Riley Patterson's record-setting day

Patterson's status for the game was in question after pictures circulated on social media with him in a walking boot. He said postgame that he tweaked his ankle and worried that he wouldn't play in the Cotton Bowl. Well, he did, and in spectacular fashion.

The junior set three Cotton Bowl records — most field goals (six), longest field goal (51 yards) and most points by a kicker (21). His six field goals and 21 points were new Memphis single-game records and all-time records for any bowl game.

With Memphis struggling to score touchdowns, Patterson helped carry the day. The All-AAC first-team selection finished with 10 field goals in his last three games.

Now Ryan Silverfield's work really begins

Silverfield, the new Memphis head coach, faces significant challenges this offseason. That he lost his first game ultimately won't define his tenure. But it could set off a chain reaction that could define his first full season.

OPPOSITE: Penn State's Journey Brown looks back as he rushes for a touchdown. MAX GERSH / THE COMMERCIAL APPEAL

RIGHT: Penn State Nittany Lions running back Noah Cain scores a touchdown past Memphis Tigers defensive end Bryce Huff. KEVIN JAIRAJ / USA TODAY SPORTS

BELOW RIGHT: Tigers wide receiver Kedarian Jones looks to move the ball past Penn State's John Reid (29) and Jaquan Brisker (7). MAX GERSH / THE COMMERCIAL APPEAL

BELOW: A Memphis fan looks on as the game slips away from the Tigers. MAX GERSH / THE COMMERCIAL APPEAL

Memphis quarterback Brady White draws back to pass.

Loss doesn't diminish U of M's magical year

Memphis wide receiver Damonte Coxie points to the cheering crowds Saturday as he walks off the field after the Goodyear Cotton Bowl Classic at AT&T Stadium in Arlington, Texas. Memphis lost to Penn State 53-39.

PHOTOS BY MAX GERSH/THE COMMERCIAL APPEAL

Memorable journey will define season

Mark Giannotto
Columnist
Memphis Commercial Appeal
USA TODAY NETWORK – TENN.

ARLINGTON, Texas – When it was over, when this wonderfully historic Memphis football season finished with a wonderfully historic Cotton Bowl game that featured everything but the happy ending, the Memphis football team walked over to the sea of blue in the stands. They pointed to the crowd and the crowd stood one more time, for one more standing ovation. And they kept

More inside

Memphis Tigers football fans discuss their team, city while watching Cotton Bowl. **Page 10A**

Cotton Bowl: 5 things learned as Memphis' dream season ends in a loss to Penn State. **Page 1B**

The Cotton Bowl in pictures. **Page 4B**

A disappointed Memphis fan looks on as the game slips away from the Tigers. Fans still gave the team a standing ovation after the game.

that brought the AAC championship game to Memphis for the first time. The second win over Cincinnati that brought an AAC title to Memphis for the first

country. "We did this," quarterback Brady White told his teammates as they

An $11.9M relief from hospital debt's cloud

After investigation, Methodist Le Bonheur system erases medical bills for thousands

Wendi C. Thomas
MLK50: Justice Through Journalism

This article was produced in partnership with MLK50, which is a member of the ProPublica Local Reporting Network.

ProPublica is a nonprofit newsroom that investigates abuses of power.

When Danielle Robinson got a letter in the mail from Methodist Le Bonheur Healthcare in October, she braced herself.

She'd missed a court-ordered payment to the hospital after she was laid off from her job in September.

In 2018, the massive nonprofit health care system sued her for just over $11,500 in unpaid hospital bills, plus $3,800 in attorney's fees. In April, a Shelby County General Sessions Court judge ordered her to pay $150 per month toward the debt.

If she was lucky, the envelope contained only a warning. If she wasn't, it was another attempt to garnish her paycheck, even though she wasn't even getting one.

Nervously, she opened the letter. "As of August 1, 2019," it said, "your total amount due is $0 for docket ROBINSON, and we have notified the court that this account has been paid in full."

"I had to read it a couple of times just to make sure," Robinson said. "I couldn't believe it. I went crying around the house."

Since July, the faith-based hospital system has erased at least $11.9 million in debts owed by Robinson and thousands of others like her, according to an analysis of Shelby County General Sessions Court records.

Methodist's move was prompted by a June investigation by MLK50 and ProPublica into the hospital's aggressive debt collection practices. From 2014

OPPOSITE: Memphis head coach Ryan Silverfield waves to fans and thanks them after the Tigers fell to Penn State in the Cotton Bowl Classic. MAX GERSH / THE COMMERCIAL APPEAL

A season that will last forever

BY MARK GIANNOTTO • THE COMMERCIAL APPEAL

The buses were ready to leave Liberty Bowl Memorial Stadium, and the quarterback was missing.

Brady White, wearing his new American Athletic Conference championship hat, stood just outside the Memphis football locker room answering questions from reporters. Running back Patrick Taylor Jr. was yelling his name from behind a barricade. He wanted to leave. He wanted to celebrate more.

So finally, Taylor walked up and put his arm around White's shoulder in front of the cameras.

"Breaking news!" Taylor yelled. "The Memphis Tigers just won the championship."

It was pure joy, the sort of joy every Memphis football fan felt on that magical Saturday night when the Tigers won their first outright conference title in 50 years and earned a spot in the Cotton Bowl.

But that joy quickly turned to uncertainty because of more breaking news. By Sunday, coach Mike Norvell had been introduced as Florida State's new coach. By the middle of the week, defensive coordinator Adam Fuller was reportedly headed to Florida State with him. By the end of the week, Ryan Silverfield was the program's new head coach.

It's the unfortunate side of college football. This amazing Memphis football team accomplished almost everything we dreamed it would and, right before it's set to play the biggest bowl game in program history, the dream seemed to end.

But if the path to this magical season taught us anything, whether it be the rise up from the dregs of college football to start of this decade, or the climb this particular team went on, let's not forget the ride that got us to the end.

Without the ride, you wouldn't be disappointed that Norvell left. Without the ride, you wouldn't be watching Memphis in the Cotton Bowl. Without the ride, that sheer giddiness you felt when Memphis won that AAC title wouldn't have felt the same.

Coaches and players come and go. Championships live on forever.

Net proceeds from the sales of "Mighty Roar" will be donated to the Tiger Scholarship Fund.